C-3790 CAREER EXAMINATION SERIES

This is your
PASSBOOK for...

Associate Project Manager

Test Preparation Study Guide
Questions & Answers

COPYRIGHT NOTICE

This book is SOLELY intended for, is sold ONLY to, and its use is RESTRICTED to individual, bona fide applicants or candidates who qualify by virtue of having seriously filed applications for appropriate license, certificate, professional and/or promotional advancement, higher school matriculation, scholarship, or other legitimate requirements of education and/or governmental authorities.

This book is NOT intended for use, class instruction, tutoring, training, duplication, copying, reprinting, excerption, or adaptation, etc., by:

1) Other publishers
2) Proprietors and/or Instructors of "Coaching" and/or Preparatory Courses
3) Personnel and/or Training Divisions of commercial, industrial, and governmental organizations
4) Schools, colleges, or universities and/or their departments and staffs, including teachers and other personnel
5) Testing Agencies or Bureaus
6) Study groups which seek by the purchase of a single volume to copy and/or duplicate and/or adapt this material for use by the group as a whole without having purchased individual volumes for each of the members of the group
7) Et al.

Such persons would be in violation of appropriate Federal and State statutes.

PROVISION OF LICENSING AGREEMENTS – Recognized educational, commercial, industrial, and governmental institutions and organizations, and others legitimately engaged in educational pursuits, including training, testing, and measurement activities, may address request for a licensing agreement to the copyright owners, who will determine whether, and under what conditions, including fees and charges, the materials in this book may be used them. In other words, a licensing facility exists for the legitimate use of the material in this book on other than an individual basis. However, it is asseverated and affirmed here that the material in this book CANNOT be used without the receipt of the express permission of such a licensing agreement from the Publishers. Inquiries re licensing should be addressed to the company, attention rights and permissions department.

All rights reserved, including the right of reproduction in whole or in part, in any form or by any means, electronic or mechanical, including photocopying, recording, or by any information storage and retrieval system, without permission in writing from the Publisher.

Copyright © 2024 by
National Learning Corporation

212 Michael Drive, Syosset, NY 11791
(516) 921-8888 • www.passbooks.com
E-mail: info@passbooks.com

PUBLISHED IN THE UNITED STATES OF AMERICA

PASSBOOK® SERIES

THE *PASSBOOK® SERIES* has been created to prepare applicants and candidates for the ultimate academic battlefield – the examination room.

At some time in our lives, each and every one of us may be required to take an examination – for validation, matriculation, admission, qualification, registration, certification, or licensure.

Based on the assumption that every applicant or candidate has met the basic formal educational standards, has taken the required number of courses, and read the necessary texts, the *PASSBOOK® SERIES* furnishes the one special preparation which may assure passing with confidence, instead of failing with insecurity. Examination questions – together with answers – are furnished as the basic vehicle for study so that the mysteries of the examination and its compounding difficulties may be eliminated or diminished by a sure method.

This book is meant to help you pass your examination provided that you qualify and are serious in your objective.

The entire field is reviewed through the huge store of content information which is succinctly presented through a provocative and challenging approach – the question-and-answer method.

A climate of success is established by furnishing the correct answers at the end of each test.

You soon learn to recognize types of questions, forms of questions, and patterns of questioning. You may even begin to anticipate expected outcomes.

You perceive that many questions are repeated or adapted so that you can gain acute insights, which may enable you to score many sure points.

You learn how to confront new questions, or types of questions, and to attack them confidently and work out the correct answers.

You note objectives and emphases, and recognize pitfalls and dangers, so that you may make positive educational adjustments.

Moreover, you are kept fully informed in relation to new concepts, methods, practices, and directions in the field.

You discover that you are actually taking the examination all the time: you are preparing for the examination by "taking" an examination, not by reading extraneous and/or supererogatory textbooks.

In short, this PASSBOOK®, used directedly, should be an important factor in helping you to pass your test.

ASSOCIATE PROJECT MANAGER

JOB DESCRIPTION
Associate Project Managers, under varying degrees of supervision, are responsible for project management work planning, coordinating, and directing the implementation of the design and construction of capital projects. May supervise subordinate staff. Performs related work.

EXAMPLES OF TYPICAL TASKS
Under general supervision, is responsible for planning, coordinating and directing effective and timely implementation of the design and construction of capital projects of moderate size and complexity.

Maintains a management information system to provide data for the planning and control for project development. Establishes project time and cost schedules. Determines and coordinates the activities required between the persons, agencies and departments responsible for project completion. Reviews all schedules, reports and orders prepared by consultants, contractors and agencies to assure conformance with project completion dates. Checks work performance and prepare management reports which stress significant problems. Resolves problems that arise in meeting schedules and costs. Meets with city agencies, contractors and citizen groups. Advises and makes recommendations to client agencies in formulating project needs, options, and consequences, assuring that functional requirements are adequately articulated and that proposed projects fulfill these requirements. Assists client agencies in developing scope of project, drawing upon own agency's technical resources to develop conceptual estimates and schedules. Oversees the consultant selection and contracting process, and manages these contracts, or retains in-house design and construction management staff. With the client agency, conducts a post-occupancy evaluation of facilities. Supervises subordinate employees. In the temporary absence of immediate supervisor, may assume the duties of that position. May incidentally perform duties of subordinates.

SCOPE OF THE EXAMINATION
The multiple-choice test may include questions on supervision including training, evaluating, assigning, and scheduling employees; project management including planning, scheduling, costing, submittals, budgeting, contracts, and payments; engineering and construction techniques, materials, equipment and practices; pertinent sections of applicable codes and laws; job related mathematics; report writing and record keeping; interpersonal communication; standards of proper employee conduct; and other related areas.

HOW TO TAKE A TEST

I. YOU MUST PASS AN EXAMINATION

A. WHAT EVERY CANDIDATE SHOULD KNOW

Examination applicants often ask us for help in preparing for the written test. What can I study in advance? What kinds of questions will be asked? How will the test be given? How will the papers be graded?

As an applicant for a civil service examination, you may be wondering about some of these things. Our purpose here is to suggest effective methods of advance study and to describe civil service examinations.

Your chances for success on this examination can be increased if you know how to prepare. Those "pre-examination jitters" can be reduced if you know what to expect. You can even experience an adventure in good citizenship if you know why civil service exams are given.

B. WHY ARE CIVIL SERVICE EXAMINATIONS GIVEN?

Civil service examinations are important to you in two ways. As a citizen, you want public jobs filled by employees who know how to do their work. As a job seeker, you want a fair chance to compete for that job on an equal footing with other candidates. The best-known means of accomplishing this two-fold goal is the competitive examination.

Exams are widely publicized throughout the nation. They may be administered for jobs in federal, state, city, municipal, town or village governments or agencies.

Any citizen may apply, with some limitations, such as the age or residence of applicants. Your experience and education may be reviewed to see whether you meet the requirements for the particular examination. When these requirements exist, they are reasonable and applied consistently to all applicants. Thus, a competitive examination may cause you some uneasiness now, but it is your privilege and safeguard.

C. HOW ARE CIVIL SERVICE EXAMS DEVELOPED?

Examinations are carefully written by trained technicians who are specialists in the field known as "psychological measurement," in consultation with recognized authorities in the field of work that the test will cover. These experts recommend the subject matter areas or skills to be tested; only those knowledges or skills important to your success on the job are included. The most reliable books and source materials available are used as references. Together, the experts and technicians judge the difficulty level of the questions.

Test technicians know how to phrase questions so that the problem is clearly stated. Their ethics do not permit "trick" or "catch" questions. Questions may have been tried out on sample groups, or subjected to statistical analysis, to determine their usefulness.

Written tests are often used in combination with performance tests, ratings of training and experience, and oral interviews. All of these measures combine to form the best-known means of finding the right person for the right job.

II. HOW TO PASS THE WRITTEN TEST

A. NATURE OF THE EXAMINATION

To prepare intelligently for civil service examinations, you should know how they differ from school examinations you have taken. In school you were assigned certain definite pages to read or subjects to cover. The examination questions were quite detailed and usually emphasized memory. Civil service exams, on the other hand, try to discover your present ability to perform the duties of a position, plus your potentiality to learn these duties. In other words, a civil service exam attempts to predict how successful you will be. Questions cover such a broad area that they cannot be as minute and detailed as school exam questions.

In the public service similar kinds of work, or positions, are grouped together in one "class." This process is known as *position-classification*. All the positions in a class are paid according to the salary range for that class. One class title covers all of these positions, and they are all tested by the same examination.

B. FOUR BASIC STEPS

1) Study the announcement

How, then, can you know what subjects to study? Our best answer is: "Learn as much as possible about the class of positions for which you've applied." The exam will test the knowledge, skills and abilities needed to do the work.

Your most valuable source of information about the position you want is the official exam announcement. This announcement lists the training and experience qualifications. Check these standards and apply only if you come reasonably close to meeting them.

The brief description of the position in the examination announcement offers some clues to the subjects which will be tested. Think about the job itself. Review the duties in your mind. Can you perform them, or are there some in which you are rusty? Fill in the blank spots in your preparation.

Many jurisdictions preview the written test in the exam announcement by including a section called "Knowledge and Abilities Required," "Scope of the Examination," or some similar heading. Here you will find out specifically what fields will be tested.

2) Review your own background

Once you learn in general what the position is all about, and what you need to know to do the work, ask yourself which subjects you already know fairly well and which need improvement. You may wonder whether to concentrate on improving your strong areas or on building some background in your fields of weakness. When the announcement has specified "some knowledge" or "considerable knowledge," or has used adjectives like "beginning principles of…" or "advanced … methods," you can get a clue as to the number and difficulty of questions to be asked in any given field. More questions, and hence broader coverage, would be included for those subjects which are more important in the work. Now weigh your strengths and weaknesses against the job requirements and prepare accordingly.

3) Determine the level of the position

Another way to tell how intensively you should prepare is to understand the level of the job for which you are applying. Is it the entering level? In other words, is this the position in which beginners in a field of work are hired? Or is it an intermediate or advanced level? Sometimes this is indicated by such words as "Junior" or "Senior" in the class title. Other jurisdictions use Roman numerals to designate the level – Clerk I, Clerk II, for example. The word "Supervisor" sometimes appears in the title. If the level is not indicated by the title, check the description of duties. Will you be working under very close supervision, or will you have responsibility for independent decisions in this work?

4) Choose appropriate study materials

Now that you know the subjects to be examined and the relative amount of each subject to be covered, you can choose suitable study materials. For beginning level jobs, or even advanced ones, if you have a pronounced weakness in some aspect of your training, read a modern, standard textbook in that field. Be sure it is up to date and has general coverage. Such books are normally available at your library, and the librarian will be glad to help you locate one. For entry-level positions, questions of appropriate difficulty are chosen – neither highly advanced questions, nor those too simple. Such questions require careful thought but not advanced training.

If the position for which you are applying is technical or advanced, you will read more advanced, specialized material. If you are already familiar with the basic principles of your field, elementary textbooks would waste your time. Concentrate on advanced textbooks and technical periodicals. Think through the concepts and review difficult problems in your field.

These are all general sources. You can get more ideas on your own initiative, following these leads. For example, training manuals and publications of the government agency which employs workers in your field can be useful, particularly for technical and professional positions. A letter or visit to the government department involved may result in more specific study suggestions, and certainly will provide you with a more definite idea of the exact nature of the position you are seeking.

III. KINDS OF TESTS

Tests are used for purposes other than measuring knowledge and ability to perform specified duties. For some positions, it is equally important to test ability to make adjustments to new situations or to profit from training. In others, basic mental abilities not dependent on information are essential. Questions which test these things may not appear as pertinent to the duties of the position as those which test for knowledge and information. Yet they are often highly important parts of a fair examination. For very general questions, it is almost impossible to help you direct your study efforts. What we can do is to point out some of the more common of these general abilities needed in public service positions and describe some typical questions.

1) General information

Broad, general information has been found useful for predicting job success in some kinds of work. This is tested in a variety of ways, from vocabulary lists to questions about current events. Basic background in some field of work, such as sociology or economics, may be sampled in a group of questions. Often these are principles which have become familiar to most persons through exposure rather than through formal training. It is difficult to advise you how to study for these questions; being alert to the world around you is our best suggestion.

2) Verbal ability

An example of an ability needed in many positions is verbal or language ability. Verbal ability is, in brief, the ability to use and understand words. Vocabulary and grammar tests are typical measures of this ability. Reading comprehension or paragraph interpretation questions are common in many kinds of civil service tests. You are given a paragraph of written material and asked to find its central meaning.

3) Numerical ability

Number skills can be tested by the familiar arithmetic problem, by checking paired lists of numbers to see which are alike and which are different, or by interpreting charts and graphs. In the latter test, a graph may be printed in the test booklet which you are asked to use as the basis for answering questions.

4) Observation

A popular test for law-enforcement positions is the observation test. A picture is shown to you for several minutes, then taken away. Questions about the picture test your ability to observe both details and larger elements.

5) Following directions

In many positions in the public service, the employee must be able to carry out written instructions dependably and accurately. You may be given a chart with several columns, each column listing a variety of information. The questions require you to carry out directions involving the information given in the chart.

6) Skills and aptitudes

Performance tests effectively measure some manual skills and aptitudes. When the skill is one in which you are trained, such as typing or shorthand, you can practice. These tests are often very much like those given in business school or high school courses. For many of the other skills and aptitudes, however, no short-time preparation can be made. Skills and abilities natural to you or that you have developed throughout your lifetime are being tested.

Many of the general questions just described provide all the data needed to answer the questions and ask you to use your reasoning ability to find the answers. Your best preparation for these tests, as well as for tests of facts and ideas, is to be at your physical and mental best. You, no doubt, have your own methods of getting into an exam-taking mood and keeping "in shape." The next section lists some ideas on this subject.

IV. KINDS OF QUESTIONS

Only rarely is the "essay" question, which you answer in narrative form, used in civil service tests. Civil service tests are usually of the short-answer type. Full instructions for answering these questions will be given to you at the examination. But in case this is your first experience with short-answer questions and separate answer sheets, here is what you need to know:

1) Multiple-choice Questions

Most popular of the short-answer questions is the "multiple choice" or "best answer" question. It can be used, for example, to test for factual knowledge, ability to solve problems or judgment in meeting situations found at work.

A multiple-choice question is normally one of three types—
- It can begin with an incomplete statement followed by several possible endings. You are to find the one ending which *best* completes the statement, although some of the others may not be entirely wrong.
- It can also be a complete statement in the form of a question which is answered by choosing one of the statements listed.

- It can be in the form of a problem – again you select the best answer.

Here is an example of a multiple-choice question with a discussion which should give you some clues as to the method for choosing the right answer:

When an employee has a complaint about his assignment, the action which will *best* help him overcome his difficulty is to
- A. discuss his difficulty with his coworkers
- B. take the problem to the head of the organization
- C. take the problem to the person who gave him the assignment
- D. say nothing to anyone about his complaint

In answering this question, you should study each of the choices to find which is best. Consider choice "A" – Certainly an employee may discuss his complaint with fellow employees, but no change or improvement can result, and the complaint remains unresolved. Choice "B" is a poor choice since the head of the organization probably does not know what assignment you have been given, and taking your problem to him is known as "going over the head" of the supervisor. The supervisor, or person who made the assignment, is the person who can clarify it or correct any injustice. Choice "C" is, therefore, correct. To say nothing, as in choice "D," is unwise. Supervisors have and interest in knowing the problems employees are facing, and the employee is seeking a solution to his problem.

2) True/False Questions

The "true/false" or "right/wrong" form of question is sometimes used. Here a complete statement is given. Your job is to decide whether the statement is right or wrong.

SAMPLE: A roaming cell-phone call to a nearby city costs less than a non-roaming call to a distant city.

This statement is wrong, or false, since roaming calls are more expensive.

This is not a complete list of all possible question forms, although most of the others are variations of these common types. You will always get complete directions for answering questions. Be sure you understand *how* to mark your answers – ask questions until you do.

V. RECORDING YOUR ANSWERS

Computer terminals are used more and more today for many different kinds of exams.

For an examination with very few applicants, you may be told to record your answers in the test booklet itself. Separate answer sheets are much more common. If this separate answer sheet is to be scored by machine – and this is often the case – it is highly important that you mark your answers correctly in order to get credit.

An electronic scoring machine is often used in civil service offices because of the speed with which papers can be scored. Machine-scored answer sheets must be marked with a pencil, which will be given to you. This pencil has a high graphite content which responds to the electronic scoring machine. As a matter of fact, stray dots may register as answers, so do not let your pencil rest on the answer sheet while you are pondering the correct answer. Also, if your pencil lead breaks or is otherwise defective, ask for another.

Since the answer sheet will be dropped in a slot in the scoring machine, be careful not to bend the corners or get the paper crumpled.

The answer sheet normally has five vertical columns of numbers, with 30 numbers to a column. These numbers correspond to the question numbers in your test booklet. After each number, going across the page are four or five pairs of dotted lines. These short dotted lines have small letters or numbers above them. The first two pairs may also have a "T" or "F" above the letters. This indicates that the first two pairs only are to be used if the questions are of the true-false type. If the questions are multiple choice, disregard the "T" and "F" and pay attention only to the small letters or numbers.

Answer your questions in the manner of the sample that follows:

32. The largest city in the United States is
    A. Washington, D.C.
    B. New York City
    C. Chicago
    D. Detroit
    E. San Francisco

1) Choose the answer you think is best. (New York City is the largest, so "B" is correct.)
2) Find the row of dotted lines numbered the same as the question you are answering. (Find row number 32)
3) Find the pair of dotted lines corresponding to the answer. (Find the pair of lines under the mark "B.")
4) Make a solid black mark between the dotted lines.

VI. BEFORE THE TEST

Common sense will help you find procedures to follow to get ready for an examination. Too many of us, however, overlook these sensible measures. Indeed, nervousness and fatigue have been found to be the most serious reasons why applicants fail to do their best on civil service tests. Here is a list of reminders:

- Begin your preparation early – Don't wait until the last minute to go scurrying around for books and materials or to find out what the position is all about.
- Prepare continuously – An hour a night for a week is better than an all-night cram session. This has been definitely established. What is more, a night a week for a month will return better dividends than crowding your study into a shorter period of time.
- Locate the place of the exam – You have been sent a notice telling you when and where to report for the examination. If the location is in a different town or otherwise unfamiliar to you, it would be well to inquire the best route and learn something about the building.
- Relax the night before the test – Allow your mind to rest. Do not study at all that night. Plan some mild recreation or diversion; then go to bed early and get a good night's sleep.
- Get up early enough to make a leisurely trip to the place for the test – This way unforeseen events, traffic snarls, unfamiliar buildings, etc. will not upset you.
- Dress comfortably – A written test is not a fashion show. You will be known by number and not by name, so wear something comfortable.

- Leave excess paraphernalia at home – Shopping bags and odd bundles will get in your way. You need bring only the items mentioned in the official notice you received; usually everything you need is provided. Do not bring reference books to the exam. They will only confuse those last minutes and be taken away from you when in the test room.
- Arrive somewhat ahead of time – If because of transportation schedules you must get there very early, bring a newspaper or magazine to take your mind off yourself while waiting.
- Locate the examination room – When you have found the proper room, you will be directed to the seat or part of the room where you will sit. Sometimes you are given a sheet of instructions to read while you are waiting. Do not fill out any forms until you are told to do so; just read them and be prepared.
- Relax and prepare to listen to the instructions
- If you have any physical problem that may keep you from doing your best, be sure to tell the test administrator. If you are sick or in poor health, you really cannot do your best on the exam. You can come back and take the test some other time.

VII. AT THE TEST

The day of the test is here and you have the test booklet in your hand. The temptation to get going is very strong. Caution! There is more to success than knowing the right answers. You must know how to identify your papers and understand variations in the type of short-answer question used in this particular examination. Follow these suggestions for maximum results from your efforts:

1) Cooperate with the monitor

The test administrator has a duty to create a situation in which you can be as much at ease as possible. He will give instructions, tell you when to begin, check to see that you are marking your answer sheet correctly, and so on. He is not there to guard you, although he will see that your competitors do not take unfair advantage. He wants to help you do your best.

2) Listen to all instructions

Don't jump the gun! Wait until you understand all directions. In most civil service tests you get more time than you need to answer the questions. So don't be in a hurry. Read each word of instructions until you clearly understand the meaning. Study the examples, listen to all announcements and follow directions. Ask questions if you do not understand what to do.

3) Identify your papers

Civil service exams are usually identified by number only. You will be assigned a number; you must not put your name on your test papers. Be sure to copy your number correctly. Since more than one exam may be given, copy your exact examination title.

4) Plan your time

Unless you are told that a test is a "speed" or "rate of work" test, speed itself is usually not important. Time enough to answer all the questions will be provided, but this does not mean that you have all day. An overall time limit has been set. Divide the total time (in minutes) by the number of questions to determine the approximate time you have for each question.

5) Do not linger over difficult questions

If you come across a difficult question, mark it with a paper clip (useful to have along) and come back to it when you have been through the booklet. One caution if you do this – be sure to skip a number on your answer sheet as well. Check often to be sure that you have not lost your place and that you are marking in the row numbered the same as the question you are answering.

6) Read the questions

Be sure you know what the question asks! Many capable people are unsuccessful because they failed to *read* the questions correctly.

7) Answer all questions

Unless you have been instructed that a penalty will be deducted for incorrect answers, it is better to guess than to omit a question.

8) Speed tests

It is often better NOT to guess on speed tests. It has been found that on timed tests people are tempted to spend the last few seconds before time is called in marking answers at random – without even reading them – in the hope of picking up a few extra points. To discourage this practice, the instructions may warn you that your score will be "corrected" for guessing. That is, a penalty will be applied. The incorrect answers will be deducted from the correct ones, or some other penalty formula will be used.

9) Review your answers

If you finish before time is called, go back to the questions you guessed or omitted to give them further thought. Review other answers if you have time.

10) Return your test materials

If you are ready to leave before others have finished or time is called, take ALL your materials to the monitor and leave quietly. Never take any test material with you. The monitor can discover whose papers are not complete, and taking a test booklet may be grounds for disqualification.

VIII. EXAMINATION TECHNIQUES

1) Read the general instructions carefully. These are usually printed on the first page of the exam booklet. As a rule, these instructions refer to the timing of the examination; the fact that you should not start work until the signal and must stop work at a signal, etc. If there are any *special* instructions, such as a choice of questions to be answered, make sure that you note this instruction carefully.

2) When you are ready to start work on the examination, that is as soon as the signal has been given, read the instructions to each question booklet, underline any key words or phrases, such as *least, best, outline, describe* and the like. In this way you will tend to answer as requested rather than discover on reviewing your paper that you *listed without describing*, that you selected the *worst* choice rather than the *best* choice, etc.

3) If the examination is of the objective or multiple-choice type – that is, each question will also give a series of possible answers: A, B, C or D, and you are called upon to select the best answer and write the letter next to that answer on your answer paper – it is advisable to start answering each question in turn. There may be anywhere from 50 to 100 such questions in the three or four hours allotted and you can see how much time would be taken if you read through all the questions before beginning to answer any. Furthermore, if you come across a question or group of questions which you know would be difficult to answer, it would undoubtedly affect your handling of all the other questions.

4) If the examination is of the essay type and contains but a few questions, it is a moot point as to whether you should read all the questions before starting to answer any one. Of course, if you are given a choice – say five out of seven and the like – then it is essential to read all the questions so you can eliminate the two that are most difficult. If, however, you are asked to answer all the questions, there may be danger in trying to answer the easiest one first because you may find that you will spend too much time on it. The best technique is to answer the first question, then proceed to the second, etc.

5) Time your answers. Before the exam begins, write down the time it started, then add the time allowed for the examination and write down the time it must be completed, then divide the time available somewhat as follows:
   - If 3-1/2 hours are allowed, that would be 210 minutes. If you have 80 objective-type questions, that would be an average of 2-1/2 minutes per question. Allow yourself no more than 2 minutes per question, or a total of 160 minutes, which will permit about 50 minutes to review.
   - If for the time allotment of 210 minutes there are 7 essay questions to answer, that would average about 30 minutes a question. Give yourself only 25 minutes per question so that you have about 35 minutes to review.

6) The most important instruction is to *read each question* and make sure you know what is wanted. The second most important instruction is to *time yourself properly* so that you answer every question. The third most important instruction is to *answer every question*. Guess if you have to but include something for each question. Remember that you will receive no credit for a blank and will probably receive some credit if you write something in answer to an essay question. If you guess a letter – say "B" for a multiple-choice question – you may have guessed right. If you leave a blank as an answer to a multiple-choice question, the examiners may respect your feelings but it will not add a point to your score. Some exams may penalize you for wrong answers, so in such cases *only*, you may not want to guess unless you have some basis for your answer.

7) Suggestions
   a. Objective-type questions
      1. Examine the question booklet for proper sequence of pages and questions
      2. Read all instructions carefully
      3. Skip any question which seems too difficult; return to it after all other questions have been answered
      4. Apportion your time properly; do not spend too much time on any single question or group of questions

5. Note and underline key words – *all, most, fewest, least, best, worst, same, opposite,* etc.
6. Pay particular attention to negatives
7. Note unusual option, e.g., unduly long, short, complex, different or similar in content to the body of the question
8. Observe the use of "hedging" words – *probably, may, most likely,* etc.
9. Make sure that your answer is put next to the same number as the question
10. Do not second-guess unless you have good reason to believe the second answer is definitely more correct
11. Cross out original answer if you decide another answer is more accurate; do not erase until you are ready to hand your paper in
12. Answer all questions; guess unless instructed otherwise
13. Leave time for review

  b. Essay questions
1. Read each question carefully
2. Determine exactly what is wanted. Underline key words or phrases.
3. Decide on outline or paragraph answer
4. Include many different points and elements unless asked to develop any one or two points or elements
5. Show impartiality by giving pros and cons unless directed to select one side only
6. Make and write down any assumptions you find necessary to answer the questions
7. Watch your English, grammar, punctuation and choice of words
8. Time your answers; don't crowd material

8) Answering the essay question

Most essay questions can be answered by framing the specific response around several key words or ideas. Here are a few such key words or ideas:

M's: manpower, materials, methods, money, management
P's: purpose, program, policy, plan, procedure, practice, problems, pitfalls, personnel, public relations

  a. Six basic steps in handling problems:
1. Preliminary plan and background development
2. Collect information, data and facts
3. Analyze and interpret information, data and facts
4. Analyze and develop solutions as well as make recommendations
5. Prepare report and sell recommendations
6. Install recommendations and follow up effectiveness

  b. Pitfalls to avoid
1. *Taking things for granted* – A statement of the situation does not necessarily imply that each of the elements is necessarily true; for example, a complaint may be invalid and biased so that all that can be taken for granted is that a complaint has been registered

2. *Considering only one side of a situation* – Wherever possible, indicate several alternatives and then point out the reasons you selected the best one
3. *Failing to indicate follow up* – Whenever your answer indicates action on your part, make certain that you will take proper follow-up action to see how successful your recommendations, procedures or actions turn out to be
4. *Taking too long in answering any single question* – Remember to time your answers properly

IX. AFTER THE TEST

Scoring procedures differ in detail among civil service jurisdictions although the general principles are the same. Whether the papers are hand-scored or graded by machine we have described, they are nearly always graded by number. That is, the person who marks the paper knows only the number – never the name – of the applicant. Not until all the papers have been graded will they be matched with names. If other tests, such as training and experience or oral interview ratings have been given, scores will be combined. Different parts of the examination usually have different weights. For example, the written test might count 60 percent of the final grade, and a rating of training and experience 40 percent. In many jurisdictions, veterans will have a certain number of points added to their grades.

After the final grade has been determined, the names are placed in grade order and an eligible list is established. There are various methods for resolving ties between those who get the same final grade – probably the most common is to place first the name of the person whose application was received first. Job offers are made from the eligible list in the order the names appear on it. You will be notified of your grade and your rank as soon as all these computations have been made. This will be done as rapidly as possible.

People who are found to meet the requirements in the announcement are called "eligibles." Their names are put on a list of eligible candidates. An eligible's chances of getting a job depend on how high he stands on this list and how fast agencies are filling jobs from the list.

When a job is to be filled from a list of eligibles, the agency asks for the names of people on the list of eligibles for that job. When the civil service commission receives this request, it sends to the agency the names of the three people highest on this list. Or, if the job to be filled has specialized requirements, the office sends the agency the names of the top three persons who meet these requirements from the general list.

The appointing officer makes a choice from among the three people whose names were sent to him. If the selected person accepts the appointment, the names of the others are put back on the list to be considered for future openings.

That is the rule in hiring from all kinds of eligible lists, whether they are for typist, carpenter, chemist, or something else. For every vacancy, the appointing officer has his choice of any one of the top three eligibles on the list. This explains why the person whose name is on top of the list sometimes does not get an appointment when some of the persons lower on the list do. If the appointing officer chooses the second or third eligible, the No. 1 eligible does not get a job at once, but stays on the list until he is appointed or the list is terminated.

X. HOW TO PASS THE INTERVIEW TEST

The examination for which you applied requires an oral interview test. You have already taken the written test and you are now being called for the interview test – the final part of the formal examination.

You may think that it is not possible to prepare for an interview test and that there are no procedures to follow during an interview. Our purpose is to point out some things you can do in advance that will help you and some good rules to follow and pitfalls to avoid while you are being interviewed.

What is an interview supposed to test?

The written examination is designed to test the technical knowledge and competence of the candidate; the oral is designed to evaluate intangible qualities, not readily measured otherwise, and to establish a list showing the relative fitness of each candidate – as measured against his competitors – for the position sought. Scoring is not on the basis of "right" and "wrong," but on a sliding scale of values ranging from "not passable" to "outstanding." As a matter of fact, it is possible to achieve a relatively low score without a single "incorrect" answer because of evident weakness in the qualities being measured.

Occasionally, an examination may consist entirely of an oral test – either an individual or a group oral. In such cases, information is sought concerning the technical knowledges and abilities of the candidate, since there has been no written examination for this purpose. More commonly, however, an oral test is used to supplement a written examination.

Who conducts interviews?

The composition of oral boards varies among different jurisdictions. In nearly all, a representative of the personnel department serves as chairman. One of the members of the board may be a representative of the department in which the candidate would work. In some cases, "outside experts" are used, and, frequently, a businessman or some other representative of the general public is asked to serve. Labor and management or other special groups may be represented. The aim is to secure the services of experts in the appropriate field.

However the board is composed, it is a good idea (and not at all improper or unethical) to ascertain in advance of the interview who the members are and what groups they represent. When you are introduced to them, you will have some idea of their backgrounds and interests, and at least you will not stutter and stammer over their names.

What should be done before the interview?

While knowledge about the board members is useful and takes some of the surprise element out of the interview, there is other preparation which is more substantive. It *is* possible to prepare for an oral interview – in several ways:

1) Keep a copy of your application and review it carefully before the interview

This may be the only document before the oral board, and the starting point of the interview. Know what education and experience you have listed there, and the sequence and dates of all of it. Sometimes the board will ask you to review the highlights of your experience for them; you should not have to hem and haw doing it.

2) Study the class specification and the examination announcement

Usually, the oral board has one or both of these to guide them. The qualities, characteristics or knowledges required by the position sought are stated in these documents. They offer valuable clues as to the nature of the oral interview. For example, if the job involves supervisory responsibilities, the announcement will usually indicate that knowledge of modern supervisory methods and the qualifications of the candidate as a supervisor will be tested. If so, you can expect such questions, frequently in the form of a hypothetical situation which you are expected to solve. NEVER go into an oral without knowledge of the duties and responsibilities of the job you seek.

3) Think through each qualification required

Try to visualize the kind of questions you would ask if you were a board member. How well could you answer them? Try especially to appraise your own knowledge and background in each area, *measured against the job sought*, and identify any areas in which you are weak. Be critical and realistic – do not flatter yourself.

4) Do some general reading in areas in which you feel you may be weak

For example, if the job involves supervision and your past experience has NOT, some general reading in supervisory methods and practices, particularly in the field of human relations, might be useful. Do NOT study agency procedures or detailed manuals. The oral board will be testing your understanding and capacity, not your memory.

5) Get a good night's sleep and watch your general health and mental attitude

You will want a clear head at the interview. Take care of a cold or any other minor ailment, and of course, no hangovers.

What should be done on the day of the interview?

Now comes the day of the interview itself. Give yourself plenty of time to get there. Plan to arrive somewhat ahead of the scheduled time, particularly if your appointment is in the fore part of the day. If a previous candidate fails to appear, the board might be ready for you a bit early. By early afternoon an oral board is almost invariably behind schedule if there are many candidates, and you may have to wait. Take along a book or magazine to read, or your application to review, but leave any extraneous material in the waiting room when you go in for your interview. In any event, relax and compose yourself.

The matter of dress is important. The board is forming impressions about you – from your experience, your manners, your attitude, and your appearance. Give your personal appearance careful attention. Dress your best, but not your flashiest. Choose conservative, appropriate clothing, and be sure it is immaculate. This is a business interview, and your appearance should indicate that you regard it as such. Besides, being well groomed and properly dressed will help boost your confidence.

Sooner or later, someone will call your name and escort you into the interview room. *This is it.* From here on you are on your own. It is too late for any more preparation. But remember, you asked for this opportunity to prove your fitness, and you are here because your request was granted.

What happens when you go in?

The usual sequence of events will be as follows: The clerk (who is often the board stenographer) will introduce you to the chairman of the oral board, who will introduce you to the other members of the board. Acknowledge the introductions before you sit down. Do not be surprised if you find a microphone facing you or a stenotypist sitting by. Oral interviews are usually recorded in the event of an appeal or other review.

Usually the chairman of the board will open the interview by reviewing the highlights of your education and work experience from your application – primarily for the benefit of the other members of the board, as well as to get the material into the record. Do not interrupt or comment unless there is an error or significant misinterpretation; if that is the case, do not hesitate. But do not quibble about insignificant matters. Also, he will usually ask you some question about your education, experience or your present job – partly to get you to start talking and to establish the interviewing "rapport." He may start the actual questioning, or turn it over to one of the other members. Frequently, each member undertakes the questioning on a particular area, one in which he is perhaps most competent, so you can expect each member to participate in the examination. Because time is limited, you may also expect some rather abrupt switches in the direction the questioning takes, so do not be upset by it. Normally, a board member will not pursue a single line of questioning unless he discovers a particular strength or weakness.

After each member has participated, the chairman will usually ask whether any member has any further questions, then will ask you if you have anything you wish to add. Unless you are expecting this question, it may floor you. Worse, it may start you off on an extended, extemporaneous speech. The board is not usually seeking more information. The question is principally to offer you a last opportunity to present further qualifications or to indicate that you have nothing to add. So, if you feel that a significant qualification or characteristic has been overlooked, it is proper to point it out in a sentence or so. Do not compliment the board on the thoroughness of their examination – they have been sketchy, and you know it. If you wish, merely say, "No thank you, I have nothing further to add." This is a point where you can "talk yourself out" of a good impression or fail to present an important bit of information. Remember, *you close the interview yourself*.

The chairman will then say, "That is all, Mr. _____, thank you." Do not be startled; the interview is over, and quicker than you think. Thank him, gather your belongings and take your leave. Save your sigh of relief for the other side of the door.

How to put your best foot forward

Throughout this entire process, you may feel that the board individually and collectively is trying to pierce your defenses, seek out your hidden weaknesses and embarrass and confuse you. Actually, this is not true. They are obliged to make an appraisal of your qualifications for the job you are seeking, and they want to see you in your best light. Remember, they must interview all candidates and a non-cooperative candidate may become a failure in spite of their best efforts to bring out his qualifications. Here are 15 suggestions that will help you:

1) Be natural – Keep your attitude confident, not cocky

If you are not confident that you can do the job, do not expect the board to be. Do not apologize for your weaknesses, try to bring out your strong points. The board is interested in a positive, not negative, presentation. Cockiness will antagonize any board member and make him wonder if you are covering up a weakness by a false show of strength.

2) Get comfortable, but don't lounge or sprawl

Sit erectly but not stiffly. A careless posture may lead the board to conclude that you are careless in other things, or at least that you are not impressed by the importance of the occasion. Either conclusion is natural, even if incorrect. Do not fuss with your clothing, a pencil or an ashtray. Your hands may occasionally be useful to emphasize a point; do not let them become a point of distraction.

3) Do not wisecrack or make small talk

This is a serious situation, and your attitude should show that you consider it as such. Further, the time of the board is limited – they do not want to waste it, and neither should you.

4) Do not exaggerate your experience or abilities

In the first place, from information in the application or other interviews and sources, the board may know more about you than you think. Secondly, you probably will not get away with it. An experienced board is rather adept at spotting such a situation, so do not take the chance.

5) If you know a board member, do not make a point of it, yet do not hide it

Certainly you are not fooling him, and probably not the other members of the board. Do not try to take advantage of your acquaintanceship – it will probably do you little good.

6) Do not dominate the interview

Let the board do that. They will give you the clues – do not assume that you have to do all the talking. Realize that the board has a number of questions to ask you, and do not try to take up all the interview time by showing off your extensive knowledge of the answer to the first one.

7) Be attentive

You only have 20 minutes or so, and you should keep your attention at its sharpest throughout. When a member is addressing a problem or question to you, give him your undivided attention. Address your reply principally to him, but do not exclude the other board members.

8) Do not interrupt

A board member may be stating a problem for you to analyze. He will ask you a question when the time comes. Let him state the problem, and wait for the question.

9) Make sure you understand the question

Do not try to answer until you are sure what the question is. If it is not clear, restate it in your own words or ask the board member to clarify it for you. However, do not haggle about minor elements.

10) Reply promptly but not hastily

A common entry on oral board rating sheets is "candidate responded readily," or "candidate hesitated in replies." Respond as promptly and quickly as you can, but do not jump to a hasty, ill-considered answer.

11) Do not be peremptory in your answers

A brief answer is proper – but do not fire your answer back. That is a losing game from your point of view. The board member can probably ask questions much faster than you can answer them.

12) Do not try to create the answer you think the board member wants

He is interested in what kind of mind you have and how it works – not in playing games. Furthermore, he can usually spot this practice and will actually grade you down on it.

13) Do not switch sides in your reply merely to agree with a board member

Frequently, a member will take a contrary position merely to draw you out and to see if you are willing and able to defend your point of view. Do not start a debate, yet do not surrender a good position. If a position is worth taking, it is worth defending.

14) Do not be afraid to admit an error in judgment if you are shown to be wrong

The board knows that you are forced to reply without any opportunity for careful consideration. Your answer may be demonstrably wrong. If so, admit it and get on with the interview.

15) Do not dwell at length on your present job

The opening question may relate to your present assignment. Answer the question but do not go into an extended discussion. You are being examined for a *new* job, not your present one. As a matter of fact, try to phrase ALL your answers in terms of the job for which you are being examined.

Basis of Rating

Probably you will forget most of these "do's" and "don'ts" when you walk into the oral interview room. Even remembering them all will not ensure you a passing grade. Perhaps you did not have the qualifications in the first place. But remembering them will help you to put your best foot forward, without treading on the toes of the board members.

Rumor and popular opinion to the contrary notwithstanding, an oral board wants you to make the best appearance possible. They know you are under pressure – but they also want to see how you respond to it as a guide to what your reaction would be under the pressures of the job you seek. They will be influenced by the degree of poise you display, the personal traits you show and the manner in which you respond.

ABOUT THIS BOOK

This book contains tests divided into Examination Sections. Go through each test, answering every question in the margin. We have also attached a sample answer sheet at the back of the book that can be removed and used. At the end of each test look at the answer key and check your answers. On the ones you got wrong, look at the right answer choice and learn. Do not fill in the answers first. Do not memorize the questions and answers, but understand the answer and principles involved. On your test, the questions will likely be different from the samples. Questions are changed and new ones added. If you understand these past questions you should have success with any changes that arise. Tests may consist of several types of questions. We have additional books on each subject should more study be advisable or necessary for you. Finally, the more you study, the better prepared you will be. This book is intended to be the last thing you study before you walk into the examination room. Prior study of relevant texts is also recommended. NLC publishes some of these in our Fundamental Series. Knowledge and good sense are important factors in passing your exam. Good luck also helps. So now study this Passbook, absorb the material contained within and take that knowledge into the examination. Then do your best to pass that exam.

EXAMINATION SECTION

EXAMINATION SECTION
TEST 1

DIRECTIONS: Each question or incomplete statement is followed by several suggested answers of completions. Select the one that BEST answers the question or Complete the statement. *PRINT THE LETTER OF THE CORRECT ANSWER IN THE SPACE AT THE RIGHT.*

1. An accepted deadline for a project approaches. However, the project manager realizes only 85% of the work has been completed. The project manager then issues a change request.
   What should the change request authorize?

    A. Corrective action based on causes
    B. Escalation approval to use contingency funding
    C. Additional resources using the contingency fund
    D. Team overtime to meet schedule

    1._____

2. _____ is a valid tool or technique to assist the project manager to assure the success of the process improvement plan.

    A. Benchmarking
    B. Change control system
    C. Process analysis
    D. Configuration management system

    2._____

3. A project manager meets with the project team to review lessons learned from previous projects. In what activity is the team involved?

    A. Performance management
    B. Project team status meeting
    C. Scope identification
    D. Risk identification

    3._____

4. _____ process helps you to purchase goods from external suppliers.

    A. Quality management
    B. Procurement management
    C. Cost management
    D. Communication management

    4._____

5. Which of the following is not involved in procurement management?

    A. Review supplier performance against contract
    B. Identify and resolve supplier performance issues
    C. Communicate the status to management
    D. Manage a WBS

    5._____

6. _____ contract is advantageous to a buyer.

    A. Fixed price
    B. Cost reimbursable
    C. Time and material
    D. Fixed price plus incentive

    6._____

7. Which of the following contracts is advantageous to a seller?

   A. Fixed price
   B. Cost reimbursable
   C. Time and material
   D. Fixed price plus incentive

8. Tom is a manager of a project whose deliverable has many uncertainties associated with it. What kind of contract should he use during the procurement process?

   A. Fixed price
   B. Cost reimbursable
   C. Time and material
   D. Fixed price plus incentive

9. Cost plus _____ is not a cost-reimbursable contract.

   A. fixed fee
   B. fee
   C. fixed time
   D. incentive fee

10. _____ type of contract helps both the seller and buyer to save, if the performance criteria are exceeded.

    A. Cost plus fixed fee
    B. Cost plus fee
    C. Cost plus fixed time
    D. Cost plus incentive fee

11. A project manager with a construction company. She has to complete a project in a specified time, but does have enough time to send the job out for bids. What type of contract would save her time?

    A. Fixed price
    B. Cost reimbursable
    C. Time and material
    D. Fixed price plus incentive

12. The major type(s) of standard warranty (ies) that are used in the business environment is (are):

    A. express
    B. negotiated
    C. implied
    D. A and C

13. During contract management, the project manager must consider the

    A. acquisition process and contract administration
    B. contract administration and ecological environment
    C. ecological environment and acquisition process
    D. offer, acceptance and consideration

14. Which contract type places the most risk on the seller?   14._____

    A. Cost plus percentage fee
    B. Cost plus incentive fee
    C. Cost plus fixed fee
    D. Firm fixed price

15. Finalizing project close-out happens when a project manager   15._____

    A. archives the project records
    B. completes the contract
    C. complete lessons learned
    D. reassigns the team

16. Unit price contract is fair to both owner and contractor,   16._____

    A. as the actual volumes will be measured and paid as the work proceeds
    B. as the owner will provide bill of quantities
    C. as both are absorbing an equal amount of risk
    D. all of the above

17. Bill is the manager of a project that requires different areas of expertise.   17._____
    Which one of the following contracts should he sign?

    A. Fixed price
    B. Cost reimbursable
    C. Time and material
    D. Unit price

18. Which of the following contracts is commonly used in projects that involve pilot   18._____
    programs or harness new technologies?

    A. Fixed price
    B. Incentive
    C. Time and material
    D. Unit price

19. Procurement cycle involves all of the following steps EXCEPT   19._____

    A. supplier contract
    B. renewal
    C. sending a proposal
    D. information gathering

20. What would happen if a project manager does not take up a background review during the   20._____
    procurement process?

    A. Price might not be negotiated
    B. Credibility of the goods might not be validated
    C. Goods might not be shipped
    D. Both A and B

21. _____ is not a part of a procurement document.

    A. Buyer's commencement to the bid
    B. Summons by the financially responsible party
    C. Establishing terms and conditions of a contract
    D. Roles of responsibilities of internal team

22. Which of the following is NOT an example of a procurement document?

    A. Offers
    B. Contracts
    C. Project record archives
    D. Request for quotation

23. A project manager needs to follow _____ for a good procurement document to be drafted.

    A. clear definition of the responsibilities, rights and commitments of both parties in the contract
    B. clear definition of the nature and quality of the goods or services to be provided
    C. clear and easy to understand language
    D. all of the above

24. Which of the following is not a concern with respect to procurement management?

    A. Reassigning the team
    B. Not all goods and services that a business requires need to be purchased from outside
    C. You would need to have a good idea of what you exactly require and then go on to consider various options and alternatives
    D. You would need to consider different criteria, apart from just the cost, to finally decide on which supplier you would want to go with.

25. Source qualifications are a part of the _____ phase of Acquisition Process Cycle.

    A. post-award
    B. pre-award
    C. award
    D. origination

KEY (CORRECT ANSWERS)

1. A
2. C
3. D
4. B
5. D

6. A
7. B
8. B
9. C
10. D

11. C
12. D
13. A
14. D
15. B

16. C
17. D
18. B
19. C
20. B

21. D
22. C
23. D
24. A
25. C

TEST 2

DIRECTIONS: Each question or incomplete statement is followed by several suggested answers of completions. Select the one that BEST answers the question or Complete the statement. *PRINT THE LETTER OF THE CORRECT ANSWER IN THE SPACE AT THE RIGHT.*

1. Which of the following project tools details the project scope?　　1._____

   A. Project plan
   B. Gantt chart
   C. Milestone checklist
   D. Score cards

2. Which of the following is NOT a project tool?　　2._____

   A. Gantt chart
   B. Milestone checklist
   C. Score cards
   D. MS project

3. _____ is accompanied by project audits by a third party. As a result, non-compliance and action items are tracked.　　3._____

   A. Gantt chart
   B. Milestone checklist
   C. Project reviews
   D. Delivery reviews

4. An IT project manager, is involved in tracking his team's performance. Which tool would he use to gauge this performance?　　4._____

   A. Score cards
   B. Gantt chart
   C. Project management software
   D. Milestone checklist

5. What tool does a manager use to track the interdependencies of each project activity?　　5._____

   A. Project plan
   B. Gantt chart
   C. Project management software
   D. Milestone checklist

6. Which tool would be used for a manager to determine if he or she is on track in terms of project progress?　　6._____

   A. Project management software
   B. Delivery reviews
   C. Project reviews
   D. Milestone checklist

7. Which of the following tools is used for individual member promotion?

    A. Delivery reviews
    B. Score cards
    C. Project reviews
    D. Milestone checklist

8. Which of the following is NOT a project management process?

    A. Project planning
    B. Project initiation
    C. Project management software
    D. Closeout and evaluation

9. _____ is the phase in which the service provider proves the eligibility and ability of completing the project to the client.

    A. Pre-sale period
    B. Project execution
    C. Sign-off
    D. Closeout and evaluation

10. Controlling of the project could be done by following all of the following protocols EXCEPT

    A. communication plan
    B. quality assurance test plan
    C. test plan
    D. project plan

11. A manager wants his project to be successful and hence verifies the successful outcome of every activity leading to successful completion of the project. Which of the following activities would he use to do so?

    A. Control
    B. Test plan
    C. Project plan
    D. Validation

12. What happens during the closeout and evaluation phase?

    A. Evaluation of the entire project
    B. Hand over the implemented system
    C. Identifying mistakes and taking necessary action
    D. All of the above

13. A project manager, is conducting validation and verification functions. Which team's assistance would she need in order to do so?

    A. Quality assurance team
    B. Project team
    C. Client team
    D. Third-party vendor

14. Tracking the effort and cost of the project is done during _____.

    A. project execution
    B. control and validation
    C. closeout and evaluation
    D. communication plan

15. _____ is the entity created for governing the processes, practices, tools and other activities related to project management in an organization.

    A. Project management office
    B. Project management software
    C. Quality assurance
    D. None of the above

16. A project management office must be built with the following considerations EXCEPT

    A. process optimization
    B. productivity enhancement
    C. building the bottom line of their organization
    D. none of the above

17. An advantage of a project management office is that it

    A. helps cut down staff
    B. helps cut down resources
    C. refines the processes related to project management
    D. all of the above

18. A project management office could fail because of

    A. lack of executive management support
    B. incapability
    C. it adds figures to the bottom line of the company
    D. both A and B

19. _____ is used to analyze the difficulties that may arise due to the execution of the project.

    A. Project management office
    B. Project management triangle
    C. Both A and B
    D. None of the above

20. The three constraints in a project management triangle are _____.

    A. time, cost and scope
    B. time, resources and quality
    C. time, resources and people
    D. time, resources and cost

21. A project manager, is experiencing challenges related to project triangle and hence finds difficulty in achieving the project objectives. Which of the following skills would help her?

    A. Time management
    B. Effective communication
    C. Managing people
    D. All of the above

22. _____ is NOT a role of a project manager.

    A. Carrying out basic project tasks
    B. Keeping stakeholders informed on the project progress
    C. Defining project scope and assigning tasks to team members
    D. Setting objectives

23. Kathy is advising Nicole on the goals and challenges a project manager must consider. Which of the following should she discuss?

    A. Deadlines
    B. Client satisfaction
    C. No budget overrun
    D. All of the above

24. Team management deals with all of the following EXCEPT

    A. providing incentives and encouragement
    B. maintaining warm and friendly relationship with teammates
    C. meeting requirements of the client
    D. including them in project related decisions

25. _____ is vital to win client satisfaction.

    A. Finishing the work on scheduled time
    B. Ensuring that most standards are met
    C. Having a limited relationship with the client
    D. All of the above

KEY (CORRECT ANSWERS)

1. A
2. D
3. C
4. A
5. B

6. D
7. B
8. C
9. A
10. C

11. D
12. D
13. A
14. A
15. A

16. D
17. C
18. D
19. B
20. A

21. D
22. A
23. D
24. C
25. A

TEST 3

DIRECTIONS: Each question or incomplete statement is followed by several suggested answers of completions. Select the one that BEST answers the question or Complete the statement. *PRINT THE LETTER OF THE CORRECT ANSWER IN THE SPACE AT THE RIGHT.*

1. What type of strategy is followed by a manager before his workforce focuses on with performance? 1._____

    A. Activators
    B. Behaviors
    C. Consequences
    D. Deviators

2. _____ define how the workforce performs or behaves within the activity or situation as a result of activators or consequences. 2._____

    A. Deviators
    B. Consequences
    C. Behaviors
    D. Activators

3. _____ explain how the manager handles the workforce after the performance. 3._____

    A. Deviators
    B. Consequences
    C. Behaviors
    D. Activators

4. Which of the following is found to have a great impact on workforce behavior? 4._____

    A. Deviators
    B. Consequences
    C. Behaviors
    D. Activators

5. Nancy, an IT project manager, is keen to delegate her work. She is aware that a good manager's role is about delegating work effectively in order to complete the task. What should she consider before delegating? 5._____

    A. Delegating the work with clear instructions and expectations stated
    B. Providing enough moral support
    C. Identify individuals that are capable of carrying out a particular task
    D. All the above

6. Which of the following is NOT a tool related to controlling and assuring quality? 6._____

    A. Check sheet
    B. Cause-and-effect diagram
    C. Activators
    D. Scatter diagram

7. _____ are used for understanding business, implementation and organizational problems. 7._____

    A. Cause-and-effect diagrams
    B. Scatter diagrams
    C. Control charts
    D. Pareto charts

8. Jim is replacing the earlier project manager in the middle of the project and hard-pressed with time. He has to work on a priority basis.
   Which of the following tools would he use to identify priorities?

   A. Cause-and-effect diagram
   B. Scatter diagram
   C. Control chart
   D. Pareto chart

Questions 9-11 refer to the following chart.

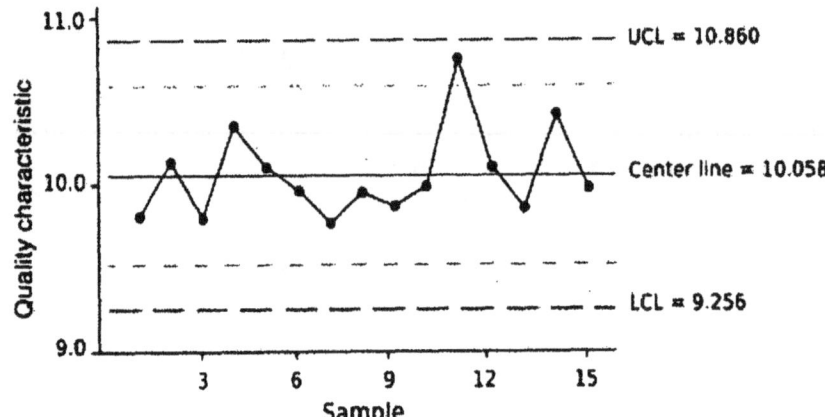

9. What type of tool is this?

   A. Control chart
   B. Flow chart
   C. Scatter diagram
   D. Pareto chart

10. The above-mentioned chart/tool is used for _____.

    A. identifying sets of priorities
    B. comparing two variables
    C. monitoring the performance of a process
    D. gathering and organizing data

11. The above chart/tool could be used to identify all of the following EXCEPT

    A. the stability of the process
    B. the common cause of variation
    C. the parameter(s) that have the highest impact on the specific concern
    D. conditions where the monitoring team needs to react

12. Which of the following tools would a project manager use to perform a trend analysis?

    A. Flow chart
    B. Scatter diagram
    C. Cause-and-effect diagram
    D. Pareto chart

13. _____ is/are a common and simple method used by project managers to arrive at an effective cause-and-effect diagram.

    A. Survey
    B. Brainstorming
    C. Informal discussions
    D. Formal presentations

14. Which of the following tools should a project manager use to gain a brief understanding of the project's critical path?

    A. Flow chart
    B. Pareto chart
    C. Histogram
    D. Check sheet

15. _____ is NOT a step involved in the benchmarking process.

    A. Planning
    B. Analysis of data
    C. Monitoring
    D. None of the above

16. As a project manager, where will you collect primary data when you collect information?

    i) Benchmarked company
    ii) Press
    iii) Publication
    iv) Website

    A. Only I
    B. Both I and II
    C. I, II, III and IV
    D. Both I and IV

17. Which of the following methods is recommended to conduct primary research?

    A. E-mail
    B. Referring to the website of other companies
    C. Telephone
    D. Face-to-face interviews

18. Analysis of data involves all of the following EXCEPT

    A. sharing data with all the stakeholders
    B. data presentation
    C. results projection
    D. classifying the performance gaps in processes

19. _____ is referred to as an enabler, which will help project managers to act wisely.

   A. Projection of results
   B. Performance gap identification
   C. Root cause of performance gaps
   D. Presentation of data

20. Which of the following needs to be done in order to monitor the quality of the project?

   A. Evaluating the progress made
   B. Reiterating the impact of change
   C. Making necessary adjustments
   D. All the above

Use the following cause-and-effect diagram to answer questions 21 through 23.

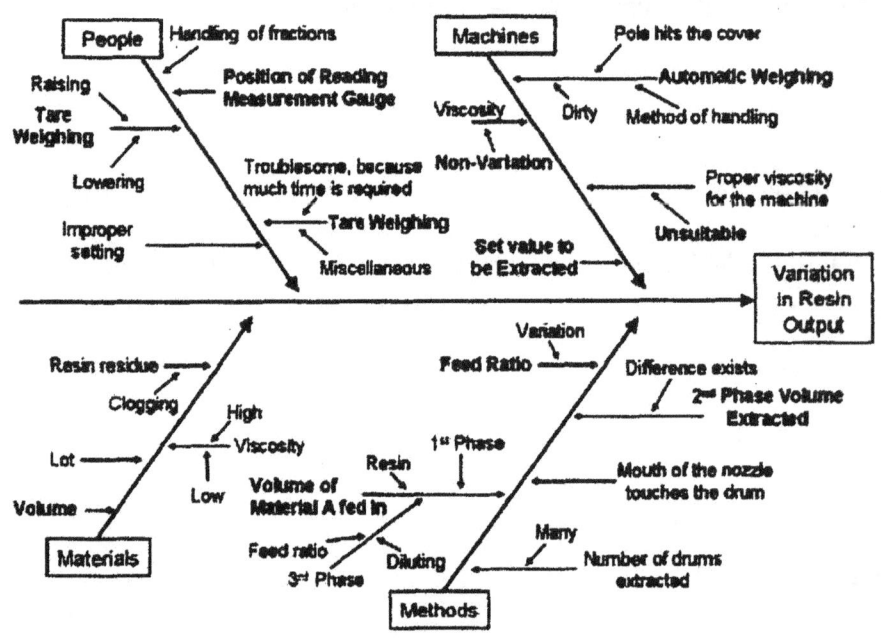

21. Which of the following is NOT represented in this diagram?

   A. Problem
   B. Major cause of the problem
   C. Contributing factors
   D. Possible causes of the problem

22. What is the effect with respect to the diagram?

   A. Materials
   B. Methods
   C. Variation in Resin Output
   D. People

23. As a project manager, what will you do to gain a better understanding of the problems and handling them? 23.____

    A. Investigations
    B. Surveys
    C. Interviews
    D. All the above

24. Kotter's change management process involves all the following steps EXCEPT 24.____

    A. building a team
    B. resource management
    C. creating a vision
    D. removing obstacles

25. _____ lets team members know why they are working on a change initiative. 25.____

    A. Removing obstacles
    B. Building a team
    C. Integrating the change
    D. Creating a vision

KEY (CORRECT ANSWERS)

1. A
2. C
3. B
4. B
5. D

6. C
7. A
8. D
9. A
10. C

11. C
12. B
13. B
14. A
15. D

16. C
17. B
18. A
19. C
20. D

21. B
22. C
23. D
24. B
25. D

TEST 4

DIRECTIONS: Each question or incomplete statement is followed by several suggested answers of completions. Select the one that best answers the question or Complete the statement. *PRINT THE LETTER OF THE CORRECT ANSWER IN THE SPACE AT THE RIGHT.*

1. Which of the following is NOT a communication blocker?
   A. Judging
   B. Accusing
   C. Globalizing
   D. Listening

2. Using words like "always" and "never" is an example of _____.
   A. judging
   B. accusing
   C. globalizing
   D. listening

3. What should you do as a project manager to eliminate communication blockers?
   A. Encourage others to avoid communication blockers by educating them
   B. Be aware of the various blockers and take steps to remove them
   C. Model to promote effective and empathetic communication
   D. All of the above

4. What would happen if there were no proper communication channel?
   A. Inefficient flow of information
   B. Clarity among employees on what is expected of them
   C. Sense of company mind/common vision among employees
   D. Clarity among employees on the happening within the company

5. As a project manager, you could use any one of the following types of language EXCEPT _____ for communicating with your team.
   A. formal
   B. insulting
   C. informal
   D. unofficial

6. A(n) _____ is/are NOT an example of formal communication.
   A. annual report
   B. business plan
   C. social gathering
   D. review meetings

7. _____ types of communication are used to communicate company policies, goals and procedures.
    A. Formal
    B. Informal
    C. Unofficial
    D. None of the above

8. _____ is NOT an example of informal communication.
    A. Survey
    B. Quality circle
    C. Team work
    D. Training program

9. "Grapevine" is an example of _____ communication.
    A. Formal
    B. Informal
    C. Unofficial
    D. None of the above

10. What question would you NOT consider as a project manager before choosing the right method to communicate?
    A. Who is the target audience?
    B. Will it lead to employee productivity?
    C. What kind of information would be helpful for clarity among employees?
    D. Which is the best way to threaten the employees?

11. Which of the following is not included in "The Five Ws of Communication Management"?
    A. What information would prompt employees to work out of fear?
    B. What information is essential for the project?
    C. What is the time required for the communication to happen effectively?
    D. Who requires information and what type of information is required?

12. _____ refers to developing a message.
    A. Decoding
    B. Encoding
    C. Transmission
    D. Feedback

13. _____ refers to interpreting the message.
    A. Decoding
    B. Encoding
    C. Transmission
    D. Feedback

14. Which of the following is not necessarily involved in a communication process?
    A. Sender
    B. Transmission
    C. Vision
    D. Receiver

15. _____ is NOT a sign of active listening.
    A. Making eye contact
    B. Asking questions to gain clarity
    C. Using gestures like nodding head
    D. Using gestures that distract the speaker

16. Madeline is a project manager and involved in conflict management. Which of the following should she use to manage a conflict?
    A. Identify actions that resolve conflicts
    B. Identify actions that would aggravate conflicts
    C. Consider different methods of resolving the conflict
    D. All the above

17. A managerial action that would NOT aggravate conflict is _____.
    A. poor communication
    B. assertive style of leadership
    C. ill-defined expectations
    D. authoritative style of leadership

18. An example of a managerial action that would NOT minimize a conflict is
    A. well-defined job descriptions
    B. participative approach
    C. submissive style of leadership
    D. fostering team spirit

19. Which of the following methods could you use as a project manager to handle conflicts?
    A. Flight
    B. Fake
    C. Fight
    D. All of the above

20. _____ is the term used when people run away from problems instead of confronting them and turn to avoidance as a means of handling conflict.
    A. Flight
    B. Fake
    C. Fight
    D. Fold

21. _____ is the term used when an individual is made to agree to a solution by means of browbeating.
    A. Flight
    B. Fake
    C. Fight
    D. Fold

22. Which of the following is NOT a step in conflict management?
    A. Choose the best solution that satisfy most people most of the time and implement this
    B. Engage in participatory dialogue and find a range of solutions that will be acceptable to all the parties concerned
    C. Eliminate those who promote mutual understanding and acceptance
    D. Identify the limiting resource or constraint that is generally at the root cause of the conflict

23. Which of the following is NOT a skill required for conflict resolution?
    A. Clarity in communication
    B. Aggressiveness
    C. Negotiation
    D. Listening

24. _____ is essential to be prepared for any problems that may arise when it is least expected.
    A. Conflict management
    B. Communication management
    C. Crisis management
    D. None of the above

25. Which of the following is NOT a type of crisis?
    A. Financial
    B. Technological
    C. Natural
    D. Negotiation

KEY (CORRECT ANSWERS)

1. D
2. C
3. D
4. A
5. B

6. C
7. A
8. A
9. C
10. D

11. A
12. B
13. A
14. C
15. D

16. D
17. B
18. C
19. D
20. A

21. D
22. C
23. B
24. C
25. D

EXAMINATION SECTION
TEST 1

DIRECTIONS: Each question or incomplete statement is followed by several suggested answers or completions. Select the one that BEST answers the question or completes the statement. *PRINT THE LETTER OF THE CORRECT ANSWER IN THE SPACE AT THE RIGHT.*

1. Management by exception (MBE) is

    A. designed to locate bottlenecks
    B. designed to pinpoint superior performance
    C. a form of index locating
    D. a form of variance reporting

2. In managerial terms, gap analysis is useful primarily in

    A. problem solving
    B. setting standards
    C. inventory control
    D. locating bottlenecks

3. ABC analysis involves

    A. problem solving
    B. indexing
    C. brainstorming
    D. inventory control

4. The Federal Discrimination in Employment Act as amended in 1978 prohibits job discrimination based on age for persons between the ages of

    A. 35 and 60   B. 40 and 65   C. 45 and 65   D. 40 and 70

5. Inspectors should be familiar with the contractor's CPM charts for a construction job primarily to determine if

    A. the job is on schedule
    B. the contractor is using the charts correctly
    C. material is on hand to keep the job on schedule
    D. there is a potential source of delay

6. The value engineering approach is frequently found in public works contracts. Value engineering is

    A. an effort to cut down or eliminate extra work payments
    B. a team approach to optimize the cost of the project
    C. to insure that material and equipment will perform as specified
    D. to insure that insurance costs on the project can be minimized

7. Historically, most costly claims have been either for

    A. unreasonable inspection requirements or unforeseen weather conditions
    B. unreasonable specification requirements or unreasonable completion time for the contract
    C. added costs due to inflation or unavailability of material
    D. delays or alleged changed conditions

8. A claim is a

    A. dispute that cannot be resolved
    B. dispute arising from ambiguity in the specifications
    C. dispute arising from the quality of the work
    D. recognition that the courts are the sole arbiters of a dispute

9. Disputes arising between a contractor and the owning agency are

    A. the result of inflexibility of either or both parties to the dispute
    B. mainly the result of shortcomings in the design
    C. the result of shortcomings in the specifications
    D. inevitable

Questions 10-13.

DIRECTIONS: Questions 10 through 13, inclusive, refers to the array of numbers listed below.

16, 7, 9, 5, 10, 8, 5, 1, 2

10. The mean of the numbers is

    A. 2   B. 5   C. 7   D. 8

11. The median of the numbers is

    A. 2   B. 5   C. 7   D. 8

12. The mode of the numbers is

    A. 2   B. 5   C. 7   D. 8

13. In statistical measurements, a subgroup that is representative of the entire group is a

    A. commutative group   B. sample
    C. central index   D. Abelian group

14. Productivity is the ratio of

    A. $\dfrac{\text{product costs}}{\text{labor costs}}$

    B. $\dfrac{\text{cost of final product}}{\text{cost of materials}}$

    C. $\dfrac{\text{outputs}}{\text{inputs}}$

    D. $\dfrac{\text{outputs cost}}{\text{time needed to product the output}}$

15. Downtime is the time a piece of equipment is

    A. idle waiting for other equipment to become available
    B. not being used for the purpose it was intended

C. being used inefficiently
D. unavailable for use

16. Index numbers   16.____

    A. relates to the cost of a product as material costs vary
    B. allows the user to find the variation from the norm
    C. are a way of comparing costs of different approaches to a problem
    D. a way of measuring and comparing changes over a period of time

17. The underlying idea behind Management by Objectives is to provide a mechanism for managers to   17.____

    A. coordinate personal and departmental plans with organizational goals
    B. motivate employees by having them participate in job decisions
    C. motivate employees by training them for the next higher position
    D. set objectives that are reasonable for the employees to attain, thus improving self-esteem among the employees

18. The ultimate objective of the project manager in planning and scheduling a project is to   18.____

    A. meet the completion dates of the project
    B. use the least amount of labor on the project
    C. use the least amount of material on the project
    D. prevent interference between the different trades

19. Scheduling with respect to the critical path method usually does not involve   19.____

    A. cost allocation
    B. starting and finishing time
    C. float for each activity
    D. project duration

20. When CPM is used on a construction project, updates are most commonly made   20.____

    A. weekly   B. every two weeks
    C. monthly   D. every two months

Questions 21-24.

DIRECTIONS: Questions 21 through 24 refer to the following network.

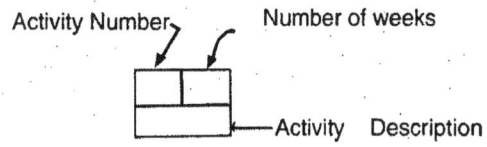

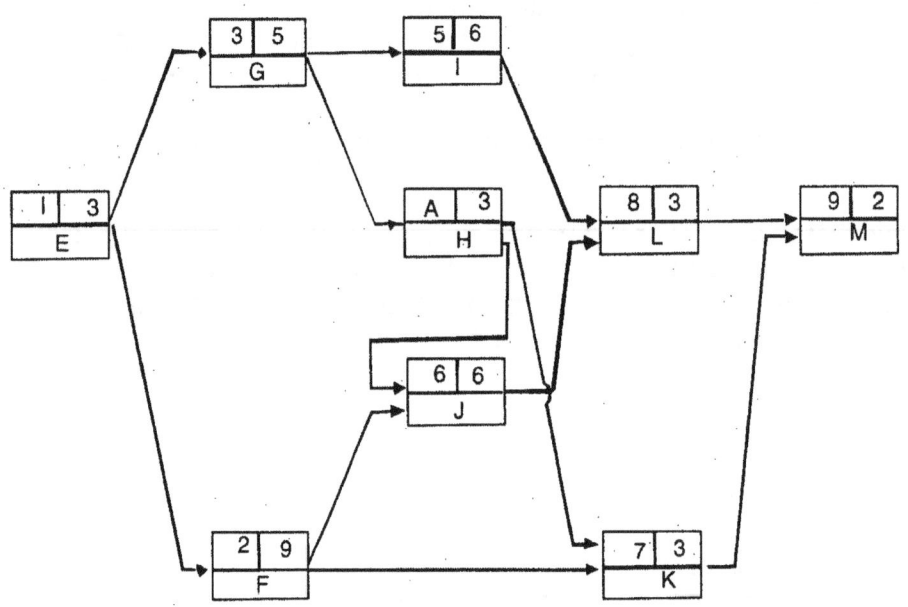

Activity Number	Activity Description	Duration in Weeks	Early Start	Early Finish	Late Start	Late Finish	Total Slack
1	E	3					
2	F	9					
3	G	5					
4	H	3					
5	I	6					
6	J	6					
7	K	3					
8	L	3					
9	M	2					

21. The critical path is

    A. E G H J L M   B. E G I L M
    C. E F J L M   D. E G H K M

21.___

22. The minimum time needed to complete the job is, in weeks,

    A. 19   B. 21   C. 22   D. 23

22.___

23. The slack time in J is, in weeks,

    A. 0   B. 1   C. 2   D. 3

23.___

24. The slack time in K is, in weeks,

    A. 4   B. 5   C. 6   D. 7

24.___

25. Of the following, the primary objective of CPM is to
    A. eliminate duplication of work
    B. overcome obstacles such as bad weather
    C. spot potential bottlenecks
    D. save on the cost of material

25.____

KEY (CORRECT ANSWERS)

1.	D	11.	C
2.	A	12.	B
3.	D	13.	B
4.	D	14.	C
5.	A	15.	D
6.	B	16.	D
7.	D	17.	A
8.	A	18.	A
9.	D	19.	A
10.	C	20.	C

21. C
22. D
23. A
24. C
25. C

TEST 2

DIRECTIONS: Each question or incomplete statement is followed by several suggested answers or completions. Select the one that BEST answers the question or completes the statement. *PRINT THE LETTER OF THE CORRECT ANSWER IN THE SPACE AT THE RIGHT.*

1. Gantt refers to

    A. bar charts
    B. milestone charts
    C. PERT networks
    D. Management by Objectives

2. PERT is an abbreviation for

    A. Progress Evaluation in Real Time
    B. Preliminary Evaluation of Running Time
    C. Program Evaluation Review Techniques
    D. Program Estimation and Repair Times

3. In project management terms, slack is equivalent to

    A. tare   B. off time   C. delay   D. float

4. The FIRST step in planning and programming a roadway pavement management system is to evaluate

    A. priorities for the work to be done
    B. the condition of your equipment
    C. the condition of the roads in the system
    D. the storage and maintenance facilities

5. Managers accomplish their work in an ever changing environment by integrating three time-tested approaches. The one of the following that is NOT a time-tested approach is

    A. scientific adaptation
    B. scientific management
    C. behavior management
    D. management sciences

6. The most effective managers manage for optimum results. This means that the manager is seeking to _____ a given situation.

    A. get the maximum results from
    B. get the most favorable results from
    C. get the most reasonable results from
    D. satisfy the conflicting interests in

7. If a manager believes that an employee is irresponsible, the employee, in subtle response to the manager's assessment, will in fact prove to be irresponsible. This is an example of a(n)

    A. conditioned reflex
    B. self-fulfilling prophesy
    C. Freudian response
    D. automatic reaction

8. Perhaps nothing distinguishes the younger generation from the older so much as the value placed on work. The older generation was generally raised to believe in the Protestant work ethic.
    This ethic holds primarily that

A. people should try to get the highest salary possible
B. work should help people to advance
C. work should be well done if it is interesting
D. work is valuable in itself and the person who does it focuses on his work

9. The standard method currently in use in inspecting bituminous paving is to inspect each activity in detail as the paving work is being installed. In recent years some agencies use a different method of inspection known as a(n)

    A. as-built quality control method
    B. statistically controlled quality assurance method
    C. data based history of previous contracts of this type
    D. performance evaluation of the completed paving contract

10. Aggregates for use in bituminous pavements should be tested for grading,

    A. abrasion, soundness, and specific gravity
    B. type of rock, abrasion, and specific gravity
    C. abrasion, soundness, and deleterious material
    D. specific gravity, chemical composition of the aggregate, and deleterious material

11. Of the following, the one that is LEAST likely to be a test for asphalt is

    A. specific gravity   B. flashpoint
    C. viscosity   D. penetration

12. According to the AASHO, for bituminous pavements PSI is an abbreviation for _____ Index.

    A. Present Serviceability   B. Pavement Smoothness
    C. Pavement Serviceability   D. Present Smoothness

13. According to the AASHO, a bituminous pavement that is in extremely poor condition will have a PSI

    A. above 5.5   B. above 3.5
    C. below 3.5   D. below 1.5

14. The U.S. Federal Highway Administration defines asphalt maintenance as including work designed primarily for rejuvenation or protection of existing surfaces less than _____ inch minimum thickness.

    A. 1/4   B. 1/2   C. 3/4   D. 1

15. The maintenance phase of a highway management system includes the establishment of a program and schedule of work based largely on budget considerations, the actual operations of crack filling, patching, etc. and

    A. inspection of completed work
    B. planning of future operations
    C. upgrading existing pavements
    D. acquisition and processing of data

16. In a bituminous asphalt pavement, the progressive separation of aggregate particles in a pavement from the surface downward or from the edges inward is the definition of

   A. alligatoring
   B. raveling
   C. scaling
   D. disintegration

17. The bituminous pavement condition for the purpose of overlay design includes ride quality, structural capacity, skid resistance, and

   A. durability
   B. age of the pavement
   C. CBR value
   D. surface distress

18. An asphalt mix is being transferred from an asphalt truck to the hopper of the paving machine. Blue smoke rises from the material being emptied into the hopper of the paving machine.
   Your conclusion should be that

   A. this is normal and is to be expected
   B. the mix is overheated
   C. the mix is too cold
   D. the mix is being transferred too rapidly

19. Polished aggregate in an asphalt pavement are aggregate particles that have been rounded and polished smooth by traffic. This is a

   A. *good* condition as it allows a smooth ride
   B. *good* condition as it preserves tires
   C. *poor* condition as it promotes skidding
   D. *poor* condition as it tends to break the bond between the asphalt and the aggregate

20. A slippery asphalt surface requires a skid-resistant surfacing material. Of the following, the cover that would be most appropriate is a(n)

   A. asphalt tack coat
   B. fog seal
   C. layer of sand rolled into the asphalt surface
   D. asphalt emulsion slurry seal

21. The maximum size of aggregate in a hot mix asphalt concrete surfacing and bases allowed by the Federal Highway Administration Grading A is _____ inch(es).

   A. 3/4   B. 1   C. 1 1/4   D. 1 1/2

22. Wet sand weighs 132 pounds per cubic foot and contains 8% noisture. The dry weight of a cubic foot of sand is _____ pounds.

   A. 122.2   B. 122.0   C. 121.7   D. 121.4

23. A very light spray application of 551h emulsified asphalt diluted with water is used on existing pavement as a seal to riinimize raveling and to enrich the surface of a dried-out pavement is known as a(n)

   A. prime coat
   B. tack coat
   C. fog seal
   D. emulsion seal

24. 90 kilometers per hour is equivalent to _____ miles per hour. 24._____

    A. 49 B. 54 C. 59 D. 64

25. In a table of pavement distress manifestations is a column broadly titled *Density of Pavement Distress*. 25._____
    This is equivalent to _____ of the defects.

    A. average depth
    B. average area
    C. extent of occurrence
    D. seriousness

KEY (CORRECT ANSWERS)

1. A	11. A
2. A	12. A
3. D	13. D
4. C	14. C
5. A	15. D
6. B	16. B
7. B	17. D
8. D	18. B
9. B	19. C
10. C	20. D

21. D
22. A
23. C
24. B
25. C

EXAMINATION SECTION
TEST 1

DIRECTIONS: Each question or incomplete statement is followed by several suggested answers or completions. Select the one that BEST answers the question or completes the statement. *PRINT THE LETTER OF THE CORRECT ANSWER IN THE SPACE AT THE RIGHT.*

1. A significant difference between ordinary contract law and construction contract law is that under most construction contracts, 1.____

    A. *breach of contract* is interpreted more widely
    B. a prime contractor's bid proposal is normally considered to be irrevocable after the bid opening and during the acceptance period prescribed in the bidding documents
    C. a subcontractor's bid is normally considered to be irrevocable even if the acceptance period is extended without his knowledge or consent
    D. an owner is not bound by oral agreements regarding the materials or workmanship of a project

2. Most negotiated construction contracts are on a _____ basis. 2.____

    A. cost-plus-fee   B. lump-sum
    C. unit-price   D. fee simple

3. When a specifier states outright the actual make, model, and catalog number of a product or the installation instructions of a manufacturer, he has written a _____ specification into the contract. 3.____

    A. reference   B. descriptive
    C. proprietary   D. performance

4. The written documents in a construction contract that describe the work to be done — including materials, equipment, construction systems, standards, and workmanship — requirements are commonly referred to as 4.____

    A. reference documents   B. drawings
    C. general conditions   D. specifications

5. According to the CSI Masterformat for specifications, each of the following would be listed in the General Requirements division of the specifications EXCEPT 5.____

    A. alternates   B. bonds and certificates
    C. maintenance   D. summary of work

6. In construction contract documents, invitations to bid are typically bound in the 6.____

    A. agreement   B. general conditions
    C. specifications   D. addenda

7. When substantial completion of a project has been achieved, it is customary for an inspection to be held to determine items that require completion or correction. The record of these items is known as a(n) 7.____

    A. supplementary condition B. punch list
    C. escalator clause   D. change order

8. The manner in which construction contracts are most commonly terminated is by

   A. full and satisfactory performance by both parties
   B. proving impossibility of performance
   C. breach of contract by either party
   D. mutual agreement of both parties

9. On a unit-price project, a bid in which each bid item includes its own direct project cost plus its pro rata share of the project overhead, markup, bond, and tax is referred to as

   A. balanced   B. bonded
   C. weighted   D. cost-plus-percentage

10. Extensions of time in construction contracts are typically formalized by an instrument known as a(n)

    A. change order   B. squinter
    C. supplementary condition D. easement

11. Under the terms of most cost-plus contracts, a common contract provision is for

    A. weekly or biweekly reimbursement of payrolls, and monthly reimbursement of all other costs, including a pro rata share of the contractor's fee
    B. monthly reimbursement of all costs including payroll and a pro rata share of the fee
    C. weekly reimbursement of all costs including payroll, and a monthly pro rata installment of the contractor's fee
    D. weekly or biweekly reimbursement of payrolls, and monthly reimbursement of all other costs except any portion of the contractor's fee, which is paid in full upon substantial completion

12. When open bidding is being used, it is necessary to include a prepared proposal form with the contract documents, because it

    A. helps in itemizing unbalanced bids
    B. exposes the different unit prices used by competing bidders
    C. is required by law
    D. ensures that all bids will be prepared and evaluated on the same basis

13. Where several different kinds or classes of similar materials are used, they should be described in a manner that permits some materials to be specified for every part of the building. This technique is a system known as the

    A. residuary legatee   B. subdivision
    C. criterion reference   D. variable proviso

14. A physical aspect of a construction site that differs materially from that indicated by the contract documents, or that is of an unusual nature and differs materially from the environment normally encountered, is described in the contract as a(n)

    A. supplementary condition   B. bid point
    C. changed condition   D. estoppel

15. Which of the following is a performance specification?

    A. Ceilings will be 2' x 2' lay-in acoustical panels.
    B. The heating system shall use #6 oil and shall be a hot water system.

C. Doors and other interior woodwork will have a natural finish.
D. Contractors shall install four inch ceramic tile throughout bathroom floor area.

16. Which of the following are generally TRUE of construction contract documents?
    I. Specific provisions prevail over general provisions.
    II. The handwritten version prevails over the typewritten version.
    III. In the event that inconsistencies exist where numbers are expressed in words and figures, the numbers govern.
    IV. If a conflict exists between drawings and specifications, the drawings usually take precedence.

    The CORRECT answer is:

    A. I, II
    B. III, IV
    C. I, II, IV
    D. II, III, IV

17. For very large construction projects, an insurance program is sometimes used which combines all the interests involved in a construction project for insurance purposes with one insurer chosen by either the owner or the contractor. This type of arrangement is known as

    A. comprehensive general liability insurance
    B. umbrella excess liability coverage
    C. wrap-up insurance policy
    D. subrogation

18. In a cost-incentive contract, the most common share of savings awarded to a contractor is _____ percent.

    A. 40
    B. 50
    C. 60
    D. 75

19. In the CSI Masterformat for specifications, which of the following items would be described and listed in Division 9?

    A. Carpet
    B. Insulation
    C. Rough carpentry
    D. Pest control

20. The submission of a complimentary bid by a contractor is generally thought to be an acceptable practice when it is done for any of the following reasons EXCEPT to

    A. fix prices and make the bidding process less competitive
    B. keep the goodwill of the owner or engineer who solicits the bid
    C. please an owner-client
    D. obtain the refund of plan deposits

21. Which of the following specifications is most effectively written?

    A. Each joint must be filled solid with mortar.
    B. Each joint is to be filled solid with mortar.
    C. Each joint shall be filled solid with mortar.
    D. Fill each joint solid with mortar.

22. Which of the following is a duty of an architect-engineer under the terms of a typical construction contract?

    A. Authorizing a contractor's periodic payments
    B. Ensuring that workmanship and materials fulfill the requirements of drawings and specifications
    C. Issuing direct instructions as to the method or procedures used in construction operations
    D. Conducting property surveys that describe the project site

23. In a technical section of a construction contract, tests for soil compaction would be described in a subparagraph under the heading of

    A. materials/equipment
    B. fabrication
    C. field quality control
    D. project/site conditions

24. Which of the following is a form that authorizes a contractor to proceed with work until a formal change order can be processed?

    A. Writ of mandamus
    B. Field order
    C. Presentment
    D. Letter of intent

25. When included in a construction contract, completed operations insurance is a liability contract that covers which of the following damages?
    I. Injuries to persons
    II. Damage to property attributed to the operation
    III. Damage to the completed work itself
    The CORRECT answer is:

    A. I only
    B. III only
    C. I, II
    D. II, III

KEY (CORRECT ANSWERS)

1. B		11. A	
2. A		12. D	
3. C		13. A	
4. D		14. C	
5. B		15. B	
6. C		16. A	
7. B		17. C	
8. A		18. B	
9. A		19. A	
10. A		20. A	

21. D
22. B
23. C
24. B
25. C

TEST 2

DIRECTIONS: Each question or incomplete statement is followed by several suggested answers or completions. Select the one that BEST answers the question or completes the statement. *PRINT THE LETTER OF THE CORRECT ANSWER IN THE SPACE AT THE RIGHT.*

1. Design decisions and special project requirements recorded at the end of the design-development phase of document preparation are included in the

    A. addendum
    B. project manual
    C. outline specification
    D. supplementary conditions

2. The greatest apparent drawback to using product approval standards in the bidding of a construction project is that

    A. competition is limited
    B. the bidding period is extended
    C. bidders assume a greater risk in accepting products other than those specified
    D. relatively less flexibility

3. The general clauses of a construction contract are composed of each of the following EXCEPT

    A. specifications
    B. supplementary conditions
    C. provisions of the agreement
    D. general conditions

4. In specifications writing, the most common form of duplication is the use of a heading titled

    A. Work of Other Sections
    B. Scope of Work
    C. Work Not Included
    D. Duplication-Repetition

5. A common provision of construction contracts is that final payment is due the contractor

    A. 30 days after substantial completion
    B. at the end of the warranty period
    C. at the stated end of the contract period
    D. upon final completion

6. The MAIN advantage of the bidder's choice specification over the base bid specification is that

    A. product selection rests entirely with the architect or engineer
    B. greater competition is invited
    C. bid shopping is eliminated
    D. specifications are generally shorter

7. Sometimes, an owner will require that a contractor include in his bid a listing of the subcontractors whose bids were used in the preparation of the prime contractor's proposal. The subcontractor listing requirement is primarily used by the owner for the purpose of

    A. estimating unit prices
    B. keeping the subcontractors subject to the owners' approval
    C. determining the percentage for a cost-plus-percentage contract
    D. discouraging bid shopping by the prime contractor

8. Special warranties that are written into construction contracts typically extend a term to

   A. 1 to 5 years
   B. 5 to 10 years
   C. 2 to 20 years
   D. 2 to lifetime

9. Of the following, which most clearly is considered a general release in full by a contractor of all claims against the owner arising out of or in consequence of the work?

   A. Agreement to terminate the contract
   B. Submission to binding arbitration
   C. Acceptance of final payment
   D. Completion of the work specified in the contract

10. A project manual is typically recorded toward the final review of the _____ phase of document preparation.

    A. construction documents
    B. schematic design
    C. design-development
    D. evaluation

11. Which of the following Division headings appears EARLIEST in the CSI Masterformat of specifications?

    A. Wood and plastics
    B. Thermal and moisture protection
    C. Sitework
    D. Concrete

12. In a typical technical section, the criteria by which the subcontractor determines that the substrates to receive his work are sound, proper, and free of defects are included in the subparagraphs under the heading of

    A. examination
    B. preparation
    C. field quality control
    D. mixes

13. For a contractor, each of the following is a potential disadvantage associated with granting an extension for the owner's acceptance period EXCEPT

    A. the potential for rises in labor wages
    B. the forfeiture of bid bonds
    C. the delaying of material orders by price advances
    D. a subcontractor or supplier's unwillingness to stand by earlier price quotes

14. What is the term for bidding requirements, contract forms, contract conditions, and specifications all bound collectively?

    A. Project manual
    B. Conditions
    C. Contract forms
    D. Master documents

15. Which of the following descriptions would NOT appear in Part 1 of a technical section that follows the CSI standard format?

    A. Submittals
    B. Equipment
    C. Delivery, storage, and handling
    D. Schedules

16. Which of the following is a disadvantage associated with the cost-plus-percentage contract?

   A. There are no direct incentives for the contractor to minimize construction costs.
   B. It is not suitable for work whose scope and nature are poorly defined at the outset of operations.
   C. It is considered unsuitable for public projects.
   D. It does not offer much flexibility in handling emergency situations.

17. In construction contracts, the term of the general warranty typically does not exceed

   A. 90 days   B. 6 months   C. 1 year   D. 2 years

18. In a construction contract, what is the term for a word description of a basic trade or material installation which outlines the quality of material to be used and the quality of workmanship to be practiced in its installation?

   A. Annotated drawing   B. Technical section
   C. Standard reference   D. Specification division

19. When an addendum is added to a construction contract, which of the following elements is typically included FIRST?

   A. Date of addendum
   B. Opening remarks and instructions
   C. Addendum and addendum number
   D. Name of architect/engineer or issuing agency

20. The main DISADVANTAGE associated with the use of alternates in the bidding process is that they

   A. decrease the security of individual bids
   B. complicate the bidding process and may increase inaccuracies
   C. are only effective when they are subtractive, rather than additive
   D. do not give the owner a clear idea of how to minimize costs

21. In a technical section written to conform to the CSI standard format, Part 2 would include descriptions of

   A. preparation   B. references
   C. field quality control   D. materials

22. In a typical project manual, which of the following elements appears FIRST?

   A. Bid bond   B. Schedule of drawings
   C. Agreement   D. General conditions

23. The insurance considerations of a construction contract, especially those governing liability, are typically incorporated into the

   A. agreement   B. general conditions
   C. specifications   D. addenda

24. Written or graphic instruments issued after the execution of a contract, which alter contract documents by additions, deletions, or corrections, are known specifically as

    A. contract modifications
    B. change orders
    C. addenda
    D. supplementary conditions

25. When a progress payments are part of a construction contract, it is common for a contractor to apply for a payment
    I. when a prescribed amount of quantified construction costs have been expended
    II. on completion of designated phases of the work
    III. a prescribed number of days before it is due under the payment schedule written into the contract

    The CORRECT answer is:

    A. II *only*
    B. I or III
    C. II or III
    D. I, II, or III

KEY (CORRECT ANSWERS)

1. C
2. B
3. A
4. B
5. A

6. B
7. D
8. C
9. C
10. A

11. C
12. A
13. B
14. A
15. D

16. A
17. C
18. B
19. D
20. B

21. D
22. C
23. B
24. A
25. C

EXAMINATION SECTION
TEST 1

DIRECTIONS: Each question or incomplete statement is followed by several suggested answers or completions. Select the one that BEST answers the question or completes the statement. *PRINT THE LETTER OF THE CORRECT ANSWER IN THE SPACE AT THE RIGHT.*

1. Of the following factors, which one is LEAST important in determining the size of staff needed in conducting an organization survey?
   The

   A. effectiveness of the personnel in supplying data for the study
   B. extent of report writing anticipated
   C. number of field locations and headquarters staff units to be covered
   D. number of individuals to be interviewed as part of fact finding

2. In planning a systems survey, which one of the following is MOST important in carrying out an effective survey after the purpose and scope of the survey has been determined? The

   A. format of the survey report
   B. methods and techniques to be employed
   C. personality problems which may materialize
   D. exact starting and completion dates

3. Which of the following is the BEST way of organizing a final report?

   A. Begin and end the report with a summary of conclusions showing how conclusions were changed as a result of findings and recommendations
   B. Begin the report with an overall summary and then place findings and recommendations in several sections
   C. Intertwine findings and conclusions in such a manner as to make the report readable and interesting
   D. Place the findings and recommendations in separate sections avoiding conclusions to the maximum extent possible

4. Which of the following disadvantages is the MOST serious in making reports verbally rather than in writing?

   A. An effective analyst may not be a good public speaker.
   B. Verbal reports are conveniently forgotten.
   C. It may not generate actions and follow-through by recipients.
   D. There is a lack of permanent record to which one may later refer.

5. Following a management survey, which of the following represents the MOST serious pitfall which may be made in recommending improvements?

   A. Failure to convince people of the benefits to be derived from the recommendations
   B. Failure to freely discuss recommendations with those who must live with them
   C. Tendency of the survey team to put their own personalities into the report
   D. Tendency to deal in personalities instead of dealing with objectives and sound management practices

6. A working outline for management analysts should include all of the following EXCEPT

   A. a chronological outline of the work steps
   B. a determination of background information needed
   C. the distribution of outline to key staff and line personnel
   D. preliminary conclusions

7. Which one of the following areas is the MOST critical for an analyst during the fact-finding stage of a study?

   A. Accuracy of data appearing in reports
   B. Attitude of those being interviewed by the analyst
   C. Observations and tentative conclusions reached by the analyst
   D. Suggestions and recommendations of interviewees

8. Creating an organization embraces all of the following areas of management EXCEPT

   A. clarification of objectives
   B. determining the number of people required to man the organization
   C. establishing operating budgets to make the plan effective
   D. proper structuring of all key positions

9. In an organization, the MAJOR barrier to accepting change is the

   A. assumption by management that everyone will willingly accept change
   B. failure by management to present proposed changes in a proper fashion
   C. lack of adaptive abilities on the part of employees
   D. lack of understanding on the part of employees of sound management principles

10. A supervisor who wishes to attain established objectives should concentrate on

    A. determining whether management is operating at maximum effectiveness
    B. making suggestions for improving the organization
    C. planning work assignments
    D. securing salary increases for needy employees

11. A usually competent employee complains that he does not understand the procedures to be followed in performing a certain task although the supervisor has explained them twice and has demonstrated them.
    Of the following, the BEST course of action for the supervisor to take is to

    A. ask the employee whether he has any problems which are bothering him
    B. assign someone else to the job
    C. explain the procedures again and demonstrate at the same time
    D. have the employee perform the job while he watches and gives additional instructions

12. GENERALLY, in order to be completely qualified as a supervisor, a person

   A. should be able to perform exceptionally well at least one of the jobs he supervises and have some knowledge of the others
   B. must have an intimate working knowledge of all facets of the jobs which he supervises
   C. should know the basic principles and procedures of the jobs he supervises
   D. need know little or nothing of the jobs which he supervises as long as he knows the principles of supervision

13. Which of the following contributes MOST to the problem of waste and inefficiency in offices?

   A. Cost control is a budget function primarily.
   B. Most organizations do not have soundly conceived budgets.
   C. Procedures improvement staffs have not as yet gained acceptance among white-collar workers.
   D. Supervisors generally are uninterested in making improvements.

14. Which of the following contributes MOST to the great number of duplicate reports and double-checking procedures frequently found in offices?
    The

   A. desire for protection
   B. desire to improve problem solving
   C. intent to *manage by exception*
   D. need for budget data

15. Which one of the following BEST identifies the narrow technician as compared with the broad-gauged analyst?
    He

   A. analyzes the activities of an agency
   B. attempts to form sound relationships with departmental personnel
   C. focuses attention on forms design and appearance
   D. follows work flow from one bureau to another by charting operational steps

16. The percentage of budget funds allocated to fixed overhead costs can be MOST effectively reduced by

   A. a soundly conceived *promotion from within* policy
   B. increasing the amount of work performed
   C. relocating to areas closer to the center of cities
   D. tightening the *fixed cost* portion of the budget

17. The term *span of control* USUALLY refers to

   A. individuals reporting to a common supervisor
   B. individuals with whom one individual has contact in the course of performing his assigned duties
   C. levels of supervision in an organization
   D. percentage of time in an organization devoted to supervisory duties

18. For an analyst, which of the following is generally LEAST important in conducting a management survey?

    A. Ability of employees to understand goals of the survey
    B. Attitude of supervisors of employees
    C. Availability of employees for interviews
    D. Cooperation of employees

19. Of the following, morale in an agency is generally MOST significantly affected by

    A. agency policies and procedures
    B. agency recognition of executives supporting agency goals
    C. the extent to which an agency meets its announced goals
    D. the number of management surveys conducted in an agency

20. Which of the following BEST describes the principle of *management by exception?*

    A. Allocating executive time and effort in direct relation to the dollar values of the budget
    B. Decentralizing management and dealing primarily with problem areas
    C. Measuring only direct costs
    D. Setting goals and objectives and managing only these

21. A WEAKNESS of many budgetary systems today is that they

    A. are subjectively determined by those most directly involved
    B. focus on management weakness rather than management strength
    C. only show variable costs
    D. show in detail why losses are occurring

22. Standards on which budgets are developed should be based PRIMARILY on

    A. a general consensus
    B. agency wishes
    C. analytical studies
    D. historical performance

23. The income, cost, and expense goals making up a budget are aimed at achieving a pre-determined objective but do not necessarily measure the lowest possible costs. This is PRIMARILY so because

    A. budget committees are accounting-oriented and are not sympathetic with the supervisor's personnel problems
    B. budget committees fail to recognize the difference between direct and indirect costs
    C. the level of expenditures provided for in a budget by budget committees is frequently an arbitrary rather than a scientifically determined amount
    D. budget committees spend considerable time evaluating data to the point that the material gathered is not representative or current

24. Linear programming has all of the following characteristics EXCEPT: It
    A. is concerned with an optimum position in relation to some objective
    B. involves the selection among alternatives or the appropriate combination of alternatives
    C. not only requires that variables be qualitative but also rests on the assumption that the relations among the variables are minimized
    D. takes into account constraints or limits within which the decision is to be reached

25. In the PERT planning system, the time in which a non-critical task can slip schedule without holding up a project is USUALLY called
    A. constraint
    B. duration time
    C. dead time
    D. float or slack

26. The Produc-trol board and Schedugraphs are commercial variations of the _____ chart.
    A. flow
    B. Gantt
    C. layout
    D. multiple activity

27. The item which cannot be analyzed by such schematic techniques as the frequency polygon and the histogram is the
    A. age of accounts receivable
    B. morale and cohesiveness of work groups
    C. number of accidents in a plant
    D. wage pattern

28. An essential employee benefit of work measurement which FREQUENTLY is the key to the successful implementation of such a program is
    A. equitable work distribution
    B. facilitation of the development of budgets
    C. measurement and control of office productivity
    D. prevention of unfair work distribution

29. An organizational arrangement whereby different employees perform different work steps upon the same work items at the same time is called the _____ method.
    A. functional
    B. homogenous
    C. parallel or linear arrangement
    D. unit assembly

30. Frequently, opposition to a management survey stems from an executive's feeling that he might be considered responsible for the unsatisfactory conditions that the project is aimed at correcting.
    To overcome this type of opposition, the analyst should GENERALLY
    A. avoid the issue altogether
    B. face the situation *head on* and, if the executive is responsible, tell him so
    C. offer a reasonable explanation for those conditions early enough in the discussion to forestall any implication of criticism
    D. place the blame for the unsatisfactory conditions at the lowest level in the organization to avoid incriminating the boss

31. Which of the following situations is LEAST likely to require a management survey?

    A. Changes in policy
    B. Management requests for additional manpower
    C. Legislation mandating changes in operating procedures
    D. Significantly lower costs than anticipated

32. The efficiency of a procedure is often influenced by the practices or performance of departments that play no direct part in carrying it out.
    In view of this, the analyst must

    A. disregard the practices or performance of departments that play no direct part in the procedure
    B. do the very best job within the department studied to compensate for the outside problems
    C. ask for assistance in solving the problems created by this situation
    D. study and evaluate the external factors to the extent that they bear on the problem

33. Which one of the following is NOT a key step in staff delegation and development?

    A. Evaluation of the completed job
    B. Preparation of a subordinate to accept additional duties
    C. Review of daily progress
    D. Selection of a suitable job to be delegated

34. Which one of the following is NOT an essential characteristic of effective delegation?

    A. In delegating, the supervisor is no longer responsible.
    B. The individual to whom authority is delegated must be accountable for fulfillment of the task.
    C. The individual to whom authority is delegated must clearly understand this authority
    D. The individual to whom authority is delegated must get honest recognition for a job well done.

35. Whenever a manager must determine how long an operation should take, he is involved with the problem of setting a time standard.
    To PROPERLY set time standards, the manager must distinguish between

    A. estimation processes and evaluation processes
    B. performance of the slowest employee and performance of the fastest employee
    C. stop watch study and work sampling
    D. synthetic and arbitrary systems

36. Assuming a report is needed, which approach USUALLY facilitates implementation?
    A

    A. draft report submitted to key people for review, discussion, modification, and then resubmission in final form
    B. report in final form which sets forth alternate recommended solutions
    C. report which sets forth the problems and the recommended solution in conformance with the desires of those most directly involved
    D. visual presentation with minimal report writing

37. Of the following elements, which is the LEAST important in writing a survey report?
A

    A. definite course of action to be followed
    B. listing of benefits to be gained through implementation
    C. review of opinions as differentiated from facts
    D. summary of conclusions

38. Physical appearance and accuracy are important features in gaining acceptance to recommendations. Which one of the following might be OVERLOOKED in preparing a report which is to have wide distribution?

    A. A comprehensive index
    B. An attractive binder
    C. Proper spacing and page layout
    D. Charts and tables

39. The elimination of meaningless reports, although reducing the total information output, IMPROVES the management process by

    A. determining the number of employees required to perform the work assigned
    B. identifying the difference between direct and indirect costs
    C. increasing the effectiveness of executives
    D. limiting the budget to variable costs

40. In determining whether or not to use a computerized system as opposed to a manual system, which of the following would normally have the MOST influence on the decision? The

    A. availability of analysts and programmers to design and install the system
    B. availability of computer time
    C. basic premise that all computerized systems are superior to manual systems
    D. volume and complexity of transactions required

KEY (CORRECT ANSWERS)

1. A	11. D	21. A	31. D
2. B	12. C	22. C	32. D
3. B	13. C	23. C	33. C
4. D	14. A	24. C	34. A
5. D	15. C	25. D	35. A
6. D	16. B	26. B	36. A
7. C	17. A	27. B	37. C
8. C	18. A	28. A	38. B
9. B	19. A	29. D	39. C
10. C	20. B	30. C	40. D

TEST 2

DIRECTIONS: Each question or incomplete statement is followed by several suggested answers or completions. Select the one that BEST answers the question or completes the statement. *PRINT THE LETTER OF THE CORRECT ANSWER IN THE SPACE AT THE RIGHT*

1. The one of the following that is NOT normally involved in the development of a management information system is

    A. determination of the best method of preparing and presenting the required information
    B. determination of line and staff relationships within the various units of the organizational structure
    C. determination of what specific information is needed for decision-making and control
    D. identification of the critical aspects of the business, i.e., the end results and other elements of performance which need to be planned and controlled

2. The long-term growth in size and complexity of both business and government has increased management's dependence on more formal written summaries of operating results in place of the informal, on-the-spot observations and judgments of smaller organizations.
   In addition, there is a growing management need to

    A. increase the complexity of those phases of the management process which have previously been simplified
    B. increase the speed and accuracy of artificial intelligence
    C. measure the effectiveness of managerial performance
    D. reduce alcoholism by greatly limiting personal contacts between the various levels of management within the organization

3. Of the following, it is MOST essential that a management information system provide information needed for

    A. determining computer time requirements
    B. developing new office layouts
    C. drawing new organization charts
    D. planning and measuring results

4. The PRIMARY purpose of control reports is to

    A. compare actual performance with planned results
    B. determine staffing requirements
    C. determine the work flow
    D. develop a new budget

5. Which one of the following has the GREATEST negative impact on communications in a large organization?

    A. Delays in formulating variable policies relating to communications
    B. Failure to conduct comprehensive courses in communications skills
    C. Failure to get information to those who need it
    D. Unclear organizational objectives

6. Efficiency of an organization is significantly impacted by all of the following EXCEPT

   A. network connectivity
   B. software compatibility
   C. hardware upgrades
   D. cloud data storage

7. The type of computer configuration in which the data are processed at one time after they have been made a matter of record is known as

   A. batching   B. in line   C. off line   D. real time

8. A computer configuration system in which the input or output equipment is directly connected and operates under control of the computer is known as

   A. off line
   B. on line
   C. random access
   D. real time

9. A manager who wants to quickly analyze the output of a particular department would most likely refer to which one of the following?

   A. An Excel spreadsheet with production data logged by department
   B. Email reports submitted by department leaders
   C. Quarterly reports describing production targets and measurements
   D. An Excel spreadsheet with employee-generated survey data related to typical daily output and capabilities

10. Computers are generally considered to consist of four major sections. The one of the following which is NOT a major section is

    A. buffer
    B. control
    C. processing
    D. storage

11. Of the following, administrative control is PRIMARILY dependent upon

    A. adequate information
    B. a widespread spy network
    C. strict supervisors
    D. strong sanctions

12. Meticulous care must be exercised in writing the methodology section of the research report so that

    A. another investigator will achieve the same results if he repeats the study
    B. the interpretation of the findings cannot be challenged
    C. the report will be well balanced
    D. the rules of scientific logic are clearly indicated

13. When data are grouped into a frequency distribution, the *true mode* by definition is the _____ in the distribution.

    A. 50% point
    B. largest single range
    C. point of greatest concentration
    D. smallest single range

14. Which of the following is LEAST likely to be a potential benefit arising from the use of electronic data processing systems?

    A. Analysis of more data and analysis of data in greater depth than manual systems
    B. Increased speed and accuracy in information processing
    C. Lower capital expenditures for office equipment
    D. Reduced personnel costs in tabulating and reporting functions

15. A *grapevine* is BEST defined as

    A. a harmful method of communication
    B. a system of communication operative below the executive level
    C. an informal communication system of no functional importance to an organization
    D. the internal and non-systematic channel of communication within an organization

16. Of the following, the symbol shown at the right, as used in a systems flow chart, means

    A. document
    B. manual operation
    C. planning
    D. process

17. The mean age of a sample group drawn from population X is 37.5 years and the standard error of the mean is 5.9. There is a *99%* probability that the computed mean age of other samples drawn from population X would fall within the range of

    A. 31.6–43.4
    B. 26.0–52.7
    C. 22.2–52.8
    D. 20.0–55.0

18. After a budget has been developed, it serves to

    A. assist the accounting department in posting expenditures
    B. measure the effectiveness of department managers
    C. provide a yardstick against which actual costs are measured
    D. provide the operating department with total expenditures to date

19. In order to ensure that work measurement or time study results will be consistent from one study to another, and reflect a fair day's work, the performance of the clerks must be rated or levelled.
    Which of the following is LEAST likely to be included among the techniques for determining the performance level or for rating the study?

    A. Predetermined times
    B. Published rating tables
    C. Sampling studies
    D. Training films

20. Of the following, the BEST practice to follow when training a new employee is to

    A. encourage him to feel free to ask questions at any time
    B. immediately demonstrate how fast his job can be done so he will know what is expected of him
    C. let him watch other employees for a week or two
    D. point out mistakes after completion so he will learn by experience

21. An IMPORTANT aspect to keep in mind during the decision-making process is that

    A. all possible alternatives for attaining goals should be sought out and considered
    B. considering various alternatives only leads to confusion
    C. once a decision has been made, it cannot be retracted
    D. there is only one correct method to reach any goal

22. Implementation of accountability REQUIRES

    A. a leader who will not hesitate to take punitive action
    B. an established system of communication from the bottom to the top
    C. explicit directives from leaders
    D. too much expense to justify it

23. Of the following, the MAJOR difference between systems and procedures analysis and work simplification is:

    A. The former complicates organizational routine and the latter simplifies it
    B. The former is objective and the latter is subjective
    C. The former generally utilizes expert advice and the latter is a *do-it-yourself* improvement by supervisors and workers
    D. There is no difference other than in name

24. Systems development is concerned with providing

    A. a specific set of work procedures
    B. an overall framework to describe general relationships
    C. definitions of particular organizational functions
    D. organizational symbolism

25. Organizational systems and procedures should be

    A. developed as problems arise as no design can anticipate adequately the requirements of an organization
    B. developed jointly by experts in systems and procedures and the people who are responsible for implementing them
    C. developed solely by experts in systems and procedures
    D. eliminated whenever possible to save unnecessary expense

26. The CHIEF danger of a decentralized control system is that

    A. excessive reports and communications will be generated
    B. problem areas may not be detected readily
    C. the expense will become prohibitive
    D. this will result in too many *chiefs*

27. Of the following, management guides and controls clerical work PRINCIPALLY through

    A. close supervision and constant checking of personnel
    B. spot checking of clerical procedures
    C. strong sanctions for clerical supervisors
    D. the use of printed forms

28. Which of the following is MOST important before conducting fact-finding interviews?

    A. Becoming acquainted with all personnel to be interviewed
    B. Explaining the techniques you plan to use
    C. Explaining to the operating officials the purpose and scope of the study
    D. Orientation of the physical layout

29. Of the following, the one that is NOT essential in carrying out a comprehensive work improvement program is

    A. standards of performance
    B. supervisory training
    C. work count/task list
    D. work distribution chart

30. Which of the following control techniques is MOST useful on large, complex systems projects?

    A. A general work plan   B. Gantt chart
    C. Monthly progress report   D. PERT chart

31. The action which is MOST effective in gaining acceptance of a study by the agency which is being studied is

    A. a directive from the agency head to install a study based on recommendations included in a report
    B. a lecture-type presentation following approval of the procedures
    C. a written procedure in narrative form covering the proposed system with visual presentations and discussions
    D. procedural charts showing the *before* situation, forms, steps, etc. to the employees affected

32. Which of the following is NOT an advantage in the use of oral instructions as compared with written instructions? Oral instruction(s)

    A. can easily be changed
    B. is superior in transmitting complex directives
    C. facilitate exchange of information between a superior and his subordinate
    D. with discussions make it easier to ascertain understanding

33. Which organization principle is MOST closely related to procedural analysis and improvement?

    A. Duplication, overlapping, and conflict should be eliminated.
    B. Managerial authority should be clearly defined.
    C. The objectives of the organization should be clearly defined.
    D. Top management should be freed of burdensome detail.

34. Which one of the following is the MAJOR objective of operational audits?

    A. Detecting fraud
    B. Determining organization problems
    C. Determining the number of personnel needed
    D. Recommending opportunities for improving operating and management practices

35. Of the following, the formalization of organization structure is BEST achieved by
    A. a narrative description of the plan of organization
    B. functional charts
    C. job descriptions together with organization charts
    D. multi-flow charts

36. Budget planning is MOST useful when it achieves
    A. cost control
    B. forecast of receipts
    C. performance review
    D. personnel reduction

37. The UNDERLYING principle of sound administration is to
    A. base administration on investigation of facts
    B. have plenty of resources available
    C. hire a strong administrator
    D. establish a broad policy

38. Although questionnaires are not the best survey tool the management analyst has to use, there are times when a good questionnaire can expedite the *fact-finding* phase of a management survey.
    Which of the following should be AVOIDED in the design and distribution of the questionnaire?
    A. Questions should be framed so that answers can be classified and tabulated for analysis.
    B. Those receiving the questionnaire must be knowledgeable enough to accurately provide the information desired.
    C. The questionnaire should enable the respondent to answer in a narrative manner.
    D. The questionnaire should require a minimum amount of writing.

39. Of the following, the formula which is used to calculate the arithmetic mean from data grouped in a frequency distribution is:
    M =

    A. $\dfrac{n}{\Sigma fx}$ B. $N(\Sigma fx)$ C. $\dfrac{\Sigma fx}{N}$ D. $\dfrac{\Sigma x}{fN}$

40. Arranging large groups of numbers in frequency distributions
    A. gives a more composite picture of the total group than a random listing
    B. is misleading in most cases
    C. is unnecessary in most instances
    D. presents the data in a form whereby further manipulation of the group is eliminated

KEY (CORRECT ANSWERS)

1. B	11. A	21. A	31. C
2. C	12. A	22. B	32. B
3. D	13. C	23. C	33. A
4. A	14. C	24. B	34. D
5. C	15. D	25. B	35. C
6. C	16. B	26. B	36. A
7. A	17. C	27. D	37. A
8. B	18. C	28. C	38. C
9. A	19. C	29. B	39. C
10. A	20. A	30. D	40. A

EXAMINATION SECTION
TEST 1

DIRECTIONS: Each question or incomplete statement is followed by several suggested answers or completions. Select the one that BEST answers the question or completes the statement. *PRINT THE LETTER OF THE CORRECT ANSWER IN THE SPACE AT THE RIGHT.*

1. The budget which shows the money to be spent to build and equip a new hospital is known as the _____ budget. 1.____

    A. capital   B. expense   C. planned   D. program

2. A significant characteristic of the program budget is that it lends itself to review and analysis. 2.____
   Why?

    A. The budget has a built-in accounting system that makes close control possible.
    B. The budget includes measurable objectives.
    C. It is possible to review performance based on units of service.
    D. All of the above

3. The advantages of program budgeting over line item and performance budgeting is: 3.____
    I. Tight, administrative control
    II. Forces the administrator to think through his total operation
    III. Measurable objectives
    IV. Simplicity of development
    V. Closer estimates of future costs

   The CORRECT answer is:

    A. I, II   B. II, III, IV
    C. II, III, V   D. III, IV, V

4. Of the following considerations, the one which is LEAST important in preparing a department budget request is the 4.____

    A. amounts in previous budget requests
    B. cost of material
    C. cost of personnel
    D. goals of the agency

5. The type of budget which provides the MOST flexibility in the use of appropriate funds is the _____ budget. 5.____

    A. accrual   B. item   C. line   D. program

6. A WEAKNESS of many budgetary systems today is that they 6.____

    A. are subjectively determined by those most directly involved
    B. focus on management weakness rather than management strength
    C. only show variable costs
    D. show in detail why losses are occurring

7. Standards on which budgets are developed should be based PRIMARILY on

   A. a general consensus
   B. agency wishes
   C. analytical studies
   D. historical performance

8. The income, cost, and expense goals making up a budget are aimed at achieving a pre-determined objective but do not necessarily measure the lowest possible costs.
   This is PRIMARILY so because

   A. budget committees are accounting-oriented and are not sympathetic with the supervisor's personnel problems
   B. budget committees fail to recognize the difference between direct and indirect costs
   C. the level of expenditures provided for in a budget by budget committees is frequently an arbitrary rather than a scientifically determined amount
   D. budget committees spend considerable time evaluating data to the point that the material gathered is not representative or current

9. You, as a unit head, have been asked to submit budget estimates of staff, equipment, and supplies in terms of programs for your unit for the coming fiscal year.
   In addition to their use in planning, such unit budget estimates can be BEST used to

   A. reveal excessive costs in operations
   B. justify increases in the debt limit
   C. analyze employee salary adjustments
   D. predict the success of future programs

10. Which of the following is the BEST reason for budgeting a new calculating machine for an office?

    A. The clerks in the office often make mistakes in adding.
    B. The machine would save time and money.
    C. It was budgeted last year but never received.
    D. All the other offices have calculating machines.

11. As an aspect of the managerial function, a budget is described BEST as a

    A. set of qualitative management controls over productivity
    B. tool based on historical accounting reports
    C. type of management plan expressed in quantitative terms
    D. precise estimate of future quantitative and qualitative contingencies

12. Which one of the following is *generally* accepted as the MAJOR immediate advantage of installing a system of program budgeting? It

    A. encourages managers to relate their decisions to the agency's long-range goals
    B. is a replacement for the financial or fiscal budget
    C. decreases the need for managers to make trade-offs in the decision-making process
    D. helps to adjust budget figures to provide for unexpected developments

13. Of the following, the BEST means for assuring necessary responsiveness of a budgetary program to changing conditions is by

    A. overestimating budgetary expenditures by 15% and assigning the excess to unforeseen problem areas
    B. underestimating budgetary expenditures by at least 20% and setting aside a reserve account in the same amount
    C. reviewing and revising the budget at regular intervals so that it retains its character as a current document
    D. establishing *budget by exception* policies for each division in the agency

14. According to expert thought in the area of budgeting, participation in the preparation of a government agency's budget should GENERALLY involve

    A. only top management
    B. only lower levels of management
    C. all levels of the organization
    D. only a central budget office or bureau

15. Of the following, the MOST useful guide to analysis of budget estimates for the coming fiscal year is a comparison with

    A. appropriations as amended for the current fiscal year
    B. manpower requirements for the previous two years
    C. initial appropriations for the current fiscal year
    D. budget estimates for the preceding five years,

16. Line managers often request more funds for their units than are actually required to attain their current objectives.
    Which one of the following is the MOST important reason for such inflated budget requests? The

    A. expectation that budget examiners will exercise their prerogative of budget cutting
    B. line manager's interest in improving the performance of his unit is thereby indicated to top management
    C. expectation that such requests will make it easier to obtain additional funds in future years
    D. opinion that it makes sense to obtain additional funds and decide later how to use them

17. Integrating budgeting with program planning and evaluation in a city agency is GENERALLY considered to be

    A. *undesirable*; budgeting must focus on the fiscal year at hand, whereas planning must concern itself with developments over a period of years
    B. *desirable*; budgeting facilitates the choice-making process by evaluating the financial implications of agency programs and forcing cost comparisons among them
    C. *undesirable*; accountants and statisticians with the required budgetary skills have little familiarity with the substantive programs that the agency is conducting
    D. *desirable*; such a partnership increases the budgetary skills of planners, thus promoting more effective use of public resources

18. In government budgeting, the problem of relating financial transactions to the fiscal year in which they are budgeted is BEST met by

    A. determining the cash balance by comparing how much money has been received and how much has been paid out
    B. applying net revenue to the fiscal year in which they are collected as offset by relevant expenses
    C. adopting a system whereby appropriations are entered when they are received and expenditures are entered when they are paid out
    D. entering expenditures on the books when the obligation to make the expenditure is made

19. If the agency's bookkeeping system records income when it is received and expenditures when the money is paid out, this system is USUALLY known as a _____ system.

    A. cash
    B. flow-payment
    C. deferred
    D. fiscal year income

20. An audit, as the term applies to budget execution, is MOST NEARLY a

    A. procedure based on the budget estimates
    B. control exercised by the executive on the legislature in the establishment of program priorities
    C. check on the legality of expenditures and is based on the appropriations act
    D. requirement which must be met before funds can be spent

21. In government budgeting, there is a procedure known as *allotment*.
    Of the following statements which relate to allotment, select the one that is MOST generally considered to be correct. Allotment

    A. increases the practice of budget units coming back to the legislative branch for supplemental appropriations
    B. is simply an example of red tape
    C. eliminates the requirement of timing of expenditures
    D. is designed to prevent waste

22. In government budgeting, the establishment of the schedules of allotments is MOST generally the responsibility of the

    A. budget unit and the legislature
    B. budget unit and the executive
    C. budget unit only
    D. executive and the legislature

23. Of the following statements relating to preparation of an organization's budget request, which is the MOST generally valid precaution?

    A. Give specific instructions on the format of budget requests and required supporting data.
    B. Because of the complexity of preparing a budget request, avoid argumentation to support the requests
    C. Put requests in whatever format is desirable.
    D. Consider that final approval will be given to initial estimates.

Question 24.

DIRECTIONS: Answer Question 24 on the basis of the following information.

Sample Budget
Environmental Safety
   Air Pollution Protection
      Personal Services $20,000,000
      Contractual Services   4,000,000
      Supplies and Materials   4,000,000
      Capital Outlay   2,000,000
         Total Air Pollution Protection $30,000,000

   Water Pollution Protection
      Personal Services $23,000,000
      Supplies and Materials   4,500,000
      Capital Outlay   20,500,000
         Total Water Pollution Protection $48,000,000
   Total Environmental Safety $78,000,000

24. Based on the above budget, which is the MOST valid statement?

   A. Environmental Safety, Air Pollution Protection, and Water Pollution Protection could all be considered program elements.
   B. The object listings included water pollution protection and capital outlay.
   C. Examples of the program element listings in the above are personal services and supplies and materials.
   D. Contractual Services and Environmental Safety were the program element listings.

25. Which of the following is NOT an advantage of a program budget over a line-item budget?
A program budget

   A. allows us to set up priority lists in deciding what activities we will spend our money on
   B. gives us more control over expenditures than a line-item budget
   C. is more informative in that we know the broad purposes of spending money
   D. enables us to see if one program is getting much less money than the others

26. Of the following statements which relate to the budget process in a well-organized government, select the one that is MOST NEARLY correct.

   A. The budget cycle is the step-by-step process which is repeated each and every fiscal year.
   B. Securing approval of the budget does not take place within the budget cycle.
   C. The development of a new budget and putting it into effect is a two-step process known as the budget cycle.
   D. The fiscal period, usually a fiscal year, has no relation to the budget cycle.

27. If a manager were asked what PPBS stands for, he would be right if he said

    A. public planning budgeting system
    B. planning programming budgeting system
    C. planning projections budgeting system
    D. programming procedures budgeting system

Questions 28-29

DIRECTIONS: Answer Questions 28 and 29 on the basis of the following information.

Sample Budget

	Amount
Refuse Collection	
Personal Services	$ 30,000
Contractual Services	5,000
Supplies and Materials	5,000
Capital Outlay	10,000
	$ 50,000
Residential Collections	
Dwellings—1 pickup per week	1,000
Tons of refuse collected per year	375
Cost of collections per ton	$ 8
Cost per dwelling pickup per year	$ 3
Total annual cost	$ 3,000

28. The sample budget shown is a simplified example of a _____ budget.

    A. factorial   B. performance
    C. qualitative   D. rational

29. The budget shown in the sample differs CHIEFLY from line-item and program budgets in that it includes

    A. objects of expenditure but not activities or functions
    B. only activities, functions, and controls
    C. activities and functions, but not objects of expenditure
    D. levels of service

30. Performance budgeting focuses PRIMARY attention upon which one of the following? The

    A. things to be acquired, such as supplies and equipment
    B. general character and relative importance of the work to be done or the service to be rendered
    C. list of personnel to be employed, by specific title
    D. separation of employee performance evaluations from employee compensation

KEY (CORRECT ANSWERS)

1.	A	16.	A
2.	B	17.	B
3.	C	18.	D
4.	A	19.	A
5.	D	20.	C
6.	A	21.	D
7.	C	22.	C
8.	C	23.	A
9.	A	24.	A
10.	B	25.	B
11.	C	26.	A
12.	A	27.	B
13.	C	28.	B
14.	C	29.	D
15.	A	30.	B

TEST 2

DIRECTIONS: Each question or incomplete statement is followed by several suggested answers or completions. Select the one that BEST answers the question or completes the statement. *PRINT THE LETTER OF THE CORRECT ANSWER IN THE SPACE AT THE RIGHT.*

1. Of the following, the FIRST step in the installation and operation of a performance budgeting system generally should be the

   A. identification of program costs in relationship to the accounting system and operating structure
   B. identification of the specific end results of past programs in other jurisdictions
   C. identification of work programs that are meaningful for management purposes
   D. establishment of organizational structures each containing only one work program

   1.____

2. Of the following, the MOST important purpose of a system of quarterly allotments of appropriated funds generally is to enable the

   A. head of the judicial branch to determine the legality of agency requests for budget increases
   B. operating agencies of government to upgrade the quality of their services without increasing costs
   C. head of the executive branch to control the rate at which the operating agencies obligate and expend funds
   D. operating agencies of government to avoid payment for services which have not been properly rendered by employees

   2.____

3. In the preparation of the agency's budget, the agency's central budget office has two responsibilities: program review and management improvement.
   Which one of the following questions concerning an operating agency's program is MOST closely related to the agency budget officer's program review responsibility?

   A. Can expenditures for supplies, materials, or equipment be reduced?
   B. Will improved work methods contribute to a more effective program?
   C. What is the relative importance of this program as compared with other programs?
   D. Will a realignment of responsibilities contribute to a higher level of program performance?

   3.____

Questions 4-9.

DIRECTIONS: Questions 4 through 9 are to be answered only on the basis of the information contained in the charts below which relate to the budget allocations of City X, a small suburban community. The charts depict the annual budget allocations by Department and by Expenditures over a five-year period.

CITY X BUDGET IN MILLIONS OF DOLLARS

TABLE I. Budget Allocations by Department

Department	2017	2018	2019	2020	2021
Public Safety	30	45	50	40	50
Health and Welfare	50	75	90	60	70
Engineering	5	8	10	5	8
Human Resources	10	12	20	10	22
Conservation and Environment	10	15	20	20	15
Education and Development	15	25	35	15	15
TOTAL BUDGET	120	180	225	150	180

TABLE II. Budget Allocations by Expenditures

Category	2017	2018	2019	2020	2021
Raw Materials and Machinery	36	63	68	30	98
Capital Outlay	12	27	56	15	18
Personal Services	72	90	101	105	64
TOTAL BUDGET	120	180	225	150	160

4. The year in which the SMALLEST percentage of the total annual budget was allocated to the Department of Education and Development is

   A. 2017   B. 2018   C. 2020   D. 2021

5. Assume that in 2020 the Department of Conservation and Environment divided its annual budget into the three categories of expenditures and in exactly the same proportion as the budget shown in Table II for the year 2020. The amount allocated for capital outlay in the Department of Conservation and Environment's 2020 budget was MOST NEARLY _____ million.

   A. $2   B. $4   C. $6   D. $10

6. From the year 2018 to the year 2020, the sum of the annual budgets for the Departments of Public Safety and Engineering showed an overall _____ million.

   A. decline of $8
   B. increase of $7
   C. decline of $15
   D. increase of $22

7. The LARGEST dollar increase in departmental budget allocations from one year to the next was in

   A. Public Safety from 2017 to 2018
   B. Health and Welfare from 2017 to 2018
   C. Education and Development from 2019 to 2020
   D. Human Resources from 2019 to 2020

8. During the five-year period, the annual budget of the Department of Human Resources was greater than the annual budget for the Department of Conservation and Environment in _____ of the years.

   A. none   B. one   C. two   D. three

9. If the total City X budget increases at the same rate from 2021 to 2022 as it did from 2020 to 2021, the total City X budget for 2022 will be MOST NEARLY _____ million.

   A. $180   B. $200   C. $210   D. $215

10. The one of the following which is LEAST important in developing a budget for the next fiscal year for project maintenance is the

   A. adequacy of the current year's budget
   B. changes in workload that can be anticipated
   C. budget restrictions indicated in a memorandum covering budget preparations
   D. staff reassignments which are expected during the next fiscal year

11. The performance budget used by the department places MOST emphasis on

   A. building facilities
   B. equipment costs
   C. personnel costs
   D. services rendered

12. The LARGEST part of the expenditures of the department is for

   A. equipment
   B. maintenance
   C. operating materials
   D. personnel services

13. The department function which requires the GREATEST expenditure of funds is

   A. refuse collection
   B. refuse disposal
   C. snow removal
   D. street cleaning

14. A FIRST step in budget preparation is *usually*

   A. a realistic attempt to satisfy all unit requests
   B. forecasting the amount of various kinds of work to be done during the coming budget year
   C. an effort to increase work output
   D. appraising the quality of work done in the previous year

15. There are various types of budgets which are used to measure different government activities.
    The type of budget which *particularly* measures input of resource as compared with output of service is the _____ budget.

   A. capital   B. traditional   C. performance   D. program

16. The budget for a given cost during a given period was $100,000. The actual cost for the period was $90,000. Based upon these facts, one should say that the responsible manager has done a better than expected job in controlling the cost if the cost is

   A. variable and actual production equaled budgeted production
   B. a discretionary fixed cost and actual production equaled budgeted production
   C. variable and actual production was 90% of budgeted production
   D. variable and actual production was 80% of budgeted production

17. In most municipal budgeting systems involving capital and operating budgets, the leasing   17._____
or renting of facilities is usually shown in

    A. the operating budget   B. the capital budget
    C. a separate schedule   D. either budget

18. New York City's budgeting procedure is unusual in that budget appropriations are consid-   18._____
ered in two parts, as follows: _____ budget and _____ budget.

    A. capital; income   B. expense; income
    C. revenue; expense   D. expense; capital

19. Budget planning is MOST useful when it achieves   19._____

    A. cost control   B. forecast of receipts
    C. performance review   D. personnel reduction

20. After a budget has been developed, it serves to   20._____

    A. assist the accounting department in posting expenditures
    B. measure the effectiveness of department managers
    C. provide a yardstick against which actual costs are measured
    D. provide the operating department with total expenditures to date

21. A budget is a plan whereby a goal is set for future operations. It affords a medium for   21._____
comparing actual expenditures with planned expenditures.
The one of the following which is the MOST accurate statement on the basis of this
statement is that

    A. the budget serves as an accurate measure of past as well as future expenditures
    B. the budget presents an estimate of expenditures to be made in the future
    C. budget estimates should be based upon past budget requirements
    D. planned expenditures usually fall short of actual expenditures

22. If one attempts to list the advantages of the management-by-exception principle as it is   22._____
used in connection with the budgeting process, several distinct advantages could be
cited.
Which of the following is NOT an advantage of this principle as it applies to the budgeting process? Management-by-exception

    A. saves time
    B. identifies critical problem areas
    C. focuses attention and concentrates effort
    D. escalates the frequency and importance of budget-related decisions

23. Of the following statements that relate to a budget, select the one that is MOST accurate.   23._____

    A. A budget is made up by an organization to plan its future activities.
    B. A budget specifies how much the organization to which it relates estimates it will
       spend over a certain period of time.
    C. A budget specifies in dollars and cents how much is spent in a particular time
       period.
    D. All plans dealing with money are budgets.

24. Of the following, the one which is NOT a contribution that a budget makes to organizational programming is that a budget

   A. enables a comparison of what actually happened with what was expected
   B. stresses the need to forecast specific goals and eliminates the need to focus on tasks needed to accomplish goals
   C. may illustrate duplication of effort between interdependent activities
   D. shows the relationship between various organizational segments

25. A line-item budget is a GOOD control budget because

   A. it clearly specifies how the items being purchased will be used
   B. expenditures can be shown primarily for contractual services
   C. it clearly specifies what the money is buying
   D. it clearly specifies the services to be provide

KEY (CORRECT ANSWERS)

1.	C	11.	D
2.	C	12.	D
3.	C	13.	A
4.	D	14.	B
5.	A	15.	C
6.	A	16.	A
7.	B	17.	A
8.	B	18.	D
9.	D	19.	A
10.	D	20.	C

21.	B
22.	D
23.	B
24.	B
25.	C

EXAMINATION SECTION
TEST 1

DIRECTIONS: Each question or incomplete statement is followed by several suggested answers or completions. Select the one that BEST answers the question or completes the statement. *PRINT THE LETTER OF THE CORRECT ANSWER IN THE SPACE AT THE RIGHT.*

1. The PRIMARY purpose of program analysis as it is used in government is to
    A. replace political judgments with rational programs and policies
    B. help decision-makers to sharpen their judgments about program choices
    C. analyze the impact of past programs on the quality of public services
    D. reduce costs by eliminating waste in public programs and services

2. While there is no complete method for program analysis that is agreed to by all the experts and is relevant to all types of problems, the MOST important element in program analysis involves the
    A. development of alternatives and the definition of objectives or criteria
    B. collection of information and the construction of a mathematical model
    C. design of experiments and procedures to validate results
    D. collection of expert opinion and the combination of their views

3. Electronic data processing is a particularly valuable tool of analysis in situations where the analyst has a processing problem involving
    A. *small* input, *few* operations, and *small* output
    B. *large* input, *many* operations, and *small* output
    C. *large* input, *few* operations, and *large* output
    D. *small* input, *many* operations, and *small* output

4. In order for an analyst to use electronic data processing to solve an analytic problem, the problem must be clearly defined.
   The BEST way to prepare material for such definition in electronic data processing is to
    A. discuss the problem with computer programmers in a meeting
    B. prepare a flow diagram outlining the steps in the analysis
    C. write a memorandum with a list of the relevant program issues
    D. write a computer program using FORTRAN, BASIC, or another language

5. The "growth rate" referred to in current political and economic discussion refers to change from year to year in a country's
    A. investments
    B. population
    C. gross national product
    D. sale of goods

6. Interactive or conversational programming is important to the program analyst ESPECIALLY for
   A. preparing analyses leading to management information systems
   B. communicating among analysts in different places
   C. using canned programs in statistical analysis
   D. testing trial solutions in rapid sequence

7. Program analysts often calls for recommendation of a choice between competing program possibilities that differ in the timing of major costs. Analysts using the present value technique by setting an interest or discount rate are in effect arguing that, other things being equal,
   A. it is inadvisable to defer the start of projects because of rising costs
   B. projects should be completed within a short time period to save money
   C. expenditures should be made out of tax revenues to avoid payment of interest
   D. postponing expenditures is advantageous at some measurable rate

8. Of the following, the formula which is MOST appropriately used to estimate the net need for a given type of service is that net need equals
   A. current clients − anticipate losses + anticipated gains
   B. $\frac{\text{current supply}}{\text{standard}}$ + current clients
   C. (client population x standard) − current supply
   D. current supply − anticipated losses + anticipated gains

9. The purpose of feasibility analysis is to protect the analyst from naïve alternatives and, MOST generally, to
   A. identify and quantify technological constraints
   B. carry out a preliminary stage of analysis
   C. anticipate potential blocks to implementation
   D. line up the support of political leadership

Questions 10-11.

DIRECTIONS: Questions 10 and 11 are to be answered on the basis of the following chart. In a hypothetical problem involving four criteria and four alternatives, the following data have been assembled.

Cost Criterion	Effectiveness Criterion	Timing Criterion	Feasibility Criterion
Alternative A $500,000	50 units	3 months	probably feasible
Alternative B $300,000	100 units	6 months	probably feasible
Alternative C $400,000	50 units	12 months	probably infeasible
Alternative D $200,000	75 units	3 months	probably infeasible

10. On the basis of the above data, it appears that the one alternative which is dominated by another alternative is Alternative
    A. A   B. B   C. C   D. D

11. If the feasibility constraint is absolute and fixed, then the critical trade-off is between lower cost
    A. on the one hand and faster timing and higher effectiveness on the other
    B. and higher effectiveness on one hand and faster timing on the other
    C. and faster timing on the one hand and higher effectiveness on the other
    D. on the one hand and higher effectiveness on the other

11.____

12. A classification of an agency's activities in a program structure is MOST useful if it highlights
    A. trade-offs that might not otherwise be considered
    B. ways to improve the efficiency of each activity
    C. the true organizational structure of an agency
    D. bases for insuring that expenditures stay within limits

12.____

13. CPM, like PERT, is a useful tool for scheduling large-scale, complex processes. In CPM, the critical path is the
    A. path composed of important links
    B. path composed of uncertain links
    C. longest path through the network
    D. shortest path through the network

13.____

14. Classical evaluative research calls for the use of control groups. However, there are practical difficulties in collecting data on individuals to be used as "controls" in program evaluations.
    Researchers may attempt to overcome these difficulties by
    A. using control groups that have no choice such as prison inmates or inmates of other public institutions or facilities
    B. developing better measures of the inputs, processes, and outputs relevant to public programs and services
    C. using experimental demonstration projects with participants in the different projects serving as comparison groups for one another
    D. abandoning attempts at formal evaluation in favor of more qualitative approaches employing a journalistic style of analysis

14.____

15. During the course of an analysis of the remaining "life" of a certain city's landfill for refuse disposal, there was a great deal of debate about the impact of changing rates of garbage generation on the amount of landfill needed and about what rates of garbage generation to expect over the next decade. Faced with the need to attempt to resolve this debate, an analyst would construct a simple model of the refuse disposal system and
    A. project landfill needs without considering refuse generation in the future
    B. conduct a detailed household survey in order to estimate future garbage generation rates
    C. ask the experts to continue to debate the issue until the argument is won by one view
    D. do a sensitivity analysis to test the impact of alternative assumptions about refuse generation

15.____

16. The limitations of traditional surveys have fostered the development and use of panels.
    A panel is a
    A. group of respondents that serves as a continuous source of survey information
    B. group of advisors expert in the design and implementation of surveys
    C. representative sample of respondents at a single point in time
    D. post-survey discussion group composed of former respondents

17. The difference between sensitivity analysis and risk analysis is that risk analysis
    A. is applicable only to profit and loss situations where the concept of risk is operable
    B. includes an estimate of probabilities of different values of input factors
    C. is applicable to physical problems while sensitivity analysis is applicable to social ones
    D. requires a computer simulation while sensitivity analysis does not

18. A decision tree, although initially applied to business problems, is a graphic device which is useful to public analysts in
    A. scheduling complex processes
    B. doing long-range forecasting
    C. formulating the structure of alternatives
    D. solving production-inventory problems

19. The purpose of a management information system in an agency is to
    A. structure data relevant to managerial decision-making
    B. put all of an agency's data in machine-processing form
    C. simplify the record-keeping operations in an agency
    D. keep an ongoing record of management's activities

20.

    [Chart: Number of responses to alarms (y-axis) vs Time (x-axis), showing "total alarms" line above "false alarms" line, both rising slightly]

    Assume that an analyst is presented with the above chart for a fire department and supplied also with information indicating a stable size firefighting staff over this time.
    The analyst could REASONABLY conclude regarding productivity that
    A. productivity over this time period was essentially stable for this firefighting force because the number of responses to real fires during this period was stable, as was the work force
    B. productivity was essentially increasing for this force because the number of total responses was increasing relative to a stable force

C. productivity was declining because a greater proportion of the total work effort was wasted effort in responding to false alarms
D. it is impossible to make a judgment about the productivity of the firefighting staff without a judgment about the value of a response to a false alarm

21. In the design of a productivity program for the sanitary department, the BEST measure of productivity would be
    A. tons of refuse collected annually
    B. number of collections made per week
    C. tons of refuse collected per truck shift
    D. number of trucks used per shift

22. The cohort-survival method for estimating future population has been widely employed.
    In this method,
    A. migration is assumed to be constant over time
    B. net migration within cohorts is assumed to be zero
    C. migration is included as a multiplier factor
    D. net migration within cohorts is assumed to be constant

23. Cost-effectiveness and cost-benefit analysis represent a systematic approach to balancing potential losses against potential gains as a prelude to public action.
    In addition to limitations based on difficulties of measurement and inadequacies in data that are typical of systematic program analysis, cost-benefit analysis suffers from a serious conceptual flaw in that
    A. the definition of benefit or cost does not typically distinguish to whom benefits or costs accrue
    B. a full-scale cost benefit analysis takes too long to do, is too expensive, and needs too much data
    C. it has been shown that such analyses are more suitable for defense or water resources problems
    D. such analyses are not useful in any problem involving capital and operating costs or benefits

24. If you were asked to develop a total cost estimate for one year for a program involving both a capital improvement and operating costs, the BEST way to estimate the capital cost component would be to
    A. divide the estimated cost of the capital improvement by the projected operating costs over the life of the improvement
    B. multiply the annual operating cost by the projected life of the capital improvement
    C. divide the amortized cost of the capital improvement by the projected life of the improvement
    D. multiply the portion of the capital improvement to be completed within the year by the cost of the improvement

25. In comparing the costs of two or more alternative programs, it is important to consider all relevant costs.
    The MOST important principle in defining "relevant cost" is that
    A. only marginal or incremental cost should be considered in the estimate
    B. only recurring costs should be considered for each alternative
    C. estimates should include the sunk costs for each alternative
    D. cost estimates need to be as precise as in budget preparation

25.____

26. Different techniques for projecting future costs may be suitable in different situations. Assume that it is necessary to estimate the future costs of maintaining garbage collection vehicles.
    Under which of the following conditions would it be advisable to develop a cost-estimating equation rather than to use unadjusted current data?
    A. When it is expected that more complex equipment will replace simpler equipment
    B. Whether or not it is expected that the nature of future garbage collection will change
    C. When the current unadjusted data still has to be verified
    D. When the nature of future garbage collection equipment is unknown

26.____

27. The following data has been collected on the costs of two pilot programs, each representing a different approach to the same problem.

	Total Cost	Fixed Cost	Variable Cost	Average Unit Cost	Number of Users
Program A	$45,000	$20,000	$50 per user	$90 Per User	500
Program B	$42,000	$7,000	$100 Per User	$120 Per User	350

Assume that the pilot programs are extended city-wide and other factors are constant.
Using the above data, what would a cost analysis conclude about the relative costs of the two programs?
Program
A. B would be less costly with fewer than 300 users and Program A would be less costly with more than 300 users
B. B would be less costly with fewer than 260 users and Program A would be less costly with more than 260 users
C. A would be less costly without regard to the size of the program
D. B would be less costly without regard to the size of the program

27.____

Questions 28-30.

DIRECTIONS: Questions 28 through 30 are to be answered on the basis of the following data assembled for a cost-benefit analysis.

	Cost	Benefit
No program	0	0
Alternative W	$3,000	$6,000
Alternative X	$10,000	$17,000
Alternative Y	$17,000	$25,000
Alternative Z	$30,000	$32,000

28. From the point of view of pushing public expenditure to the point where marginal benefit equals or exceeds marginal cost, the BEST alternative is Alternative
    A. W B. X C. Y D. Z

29. From the point of view of selecting the alternative with the best cost-benefit ratio, the BEST alternative is Alternative
    A. W B. X C. Y D. Z

30. From the point of view of selecting the alternative with the best measure of net benefit, the BEST alternative is Alternative
    A. W B. X C. Y D. Z

Questions 31-35.

DIRECTIONS: The set of answers listed below applies to Questions 31 through 35. Each answer is a type of statistical test.

   A. Analysis of variance
   B. Pearson Product-Moment Correlation (r)
   C. t-test
   D. x^2 test (Chi-squared)

Pick the test which is MOST appropriate to the situation described. An answer may be used more than once.

31. A comparison between two correlated means obtained from a small sample.
    The CORRECT answer is:
    A. A B. B C. C D. D

32. A comparison of three or more means.
    The CORRECT answer is:
    A. A B. B C. C D. D

33. A comparison of the divergence of observed frequencies with those expected on the hypothesis of equal probability of occurrence.
    The CORRECT answer is:
    A. A B. B C. C D. D

34. A comparison of the divergence of observed frequencies with those expected on the hypothesis of a normal distribution.
    The CORRECT answer is:
    A. A B. B C. C D. D

35. A comparison between two uncorrelated means obtained from small samples.
    The CORRECT answer is:
    A. A B. B C. C D. D

36. There are many different models for evaluative research.
A time-series design is an example of a _____ experimental design.
   A. field   B. true   C. quasi-   D. pre-

37. In policy research, as in all kinds of research, it is important to develop research hypotheses early.
The MAIN purpose of a research hypothesis is to
   A. include the kind of statistical procedures to be used in the research
   B. provide a ready answer in case data is not available for doing research
   C. serve as a guide to the kind of data that must be collected in order to answer the research question
   D. clarify what is known and what is not known in the research problem

38. While descriptive and causal research are not completely separable, there has been a distinct effort to move in the direction of causal research.
Such an effort is epitomized by the use of
   A. predictive models and measures of deviation from predictions
   B. option and attitudinal surveys in local neighborhoods
   C. community studies and area profiles of localities
   D. individual case histories and group case studies

39. The one of the following which BEST describes a periodic report is that it
   A. provides a record of accomplishments for a given time span and a comparison with similar time spans in the past
   B. covers the progress made in a project that has been postponed
   C. integrates, summarizes, and perhaps interprets published data on technical or scientific material
   D. describes a decision, advocates a policy or action, and presents facts in support of the writer's position

40. The PRIMARY purpose of including pictorial illustrations in a formal report is usually to
   A. amplify information which has been adequately treated verbally
   B. present detail that are difficult to describe verbally
   C. provide the reader with a pleasant, momentary distraction
   D. present supplementary information incidental to the main ideas developed in the report

KEY (CORRECT ANSWERS)

1.	B	11.	B	21.	C	31.	C
2.	A	12.	A	22.	B	32.	A
3.	B	13.	C	23.	A	33.	D
4.	B	14.	C	24.	C	34.	D
5.	C	15.	D	25.	A	35.	C
6.	D	16.	A	26.	A	36.	C
7.	D	17.	B	27.	B	37.	C
8.	C	18.	C	28.	C	38.	A
9.	C	19.	A	29.	A	39.	A
10.	C	20.	D	30.	C	40.	B

TEST 2

DIRECTIONS: Each question or incomplete statement is followed by several suggested answers or completions. Select the one that BEST answers the question or completes the statement. *PRINT THE LETTER OF THE CORRECT ANSWER IN THE SPACE AT THE RIGHT.*

1. A measurement procedure is considered to be RELIABLE to the extent that
   A. independent applications under similar conditions yield consistent results
   B. independent applications under different conditions yield similar results
   C. scores reflect true differences among individuals or situations
   D. scores reflect true differences in the same individual over time

   1.____

2. Different scales of measurement are distinguished by the feasibility of various empirical operations.
   An ordinal scale of measurement
   A. is not as useful as a ratio or interval scale
   B. is useful in rank-ordering or priority setting
   C. provides the data for addition or subtraction
   D. provides the data for computation of means

   2.____

3. A widely used approach to sampling is systematic sampling, i.e., selecting every Kth element in a listing.
   Even with a random start, a DISADVANTAGE in this approach is that
   A. the listing used may contain a cyclical pattern
   B. it is too similar to a simple random sample
   C. the system does not insure a probability sample
   D. it yield an unpredictable sample size

   3.____

4. A rule of thumb sometimes used in sample size selection it to set sample size equal to five percent of the population size.
   Other things being equal, this rule
   A. tends to oversample small populations
   B. tends to oversample large populations
   C. provides an accurate rule for sampling
   D. is a relatively inexpensive basis for sampling

   4.____

5. With regard to a stratified random sample, it may be APPROPRIATE to sample the various strata in different proportions in order to
   A. approximate the characteristics of a true random sample
   B. establish classes that are internally heterogenous in each case
   C. avoid the necessity of subdividing the cases within each stratum
   D. adequately cover important strata that have small numbers of cases

   5.____

6. One possible response to the "unknown" or "no answer" category in a tabulation of survey information is to "allocate" the unknown responses, i.e., to estimate the missing data on the basis of other known information about the respondents.

   6.____

This technique is APPROPRIATE when the unknown category
- A. is very small and is randomly distributed within all subgroups of respondents
- B. is very large and is randomly distributed within all subgroups of respondents
- C. reflects an interviewing failure and a subgroup in the sample ends to produce more unknowns
- D. is a legitimate category and a subgroup in the sample tends to produce more unknowns

7. In presenting cross-tabulated data showing the relationship between two variables, it is MOST meaningful to compute percentages
    - A. in both directions in all instances
    - B. of each cell in relation to the grand total
    - C. in the direction of the smaller number of cells
    - D. in the direction of the causal factor

8. In portraying data based on a sampling operation, it is MOST meaningful and comprehensible to the reader to present
    - A. percentages for the sample and the universe
    - B. percentages by themselves
    - C. percentages and the base figures
    - D. numbers by themselves

9. A new bridge spanning a river is expected to carry 60,000 cars a day on a rainy day and 80,000 cars a day on other kinds of days.
   If there is a $5 toll and one chance in four of a rainy day, the expected value of a day's revenue is
    - A. $175,000
    - B. $375,000
    - C. $475,000
    - D. $700,000

10. The analyst who is asked to estimate the probability of a relatively rare event occurring cannot use the classical frequency measures of probability but rather should
    - A. use a random-numbers table to pick a probability
    - B. project historical data into the future
    - C. indicate that no probabilistic judgment is possible
    - D. make the best possible judgment as to the subjective probability

11. A useful source of census data for computing annual indicators is the
    - A. Public Use Sample
    - B. Continuing Population Survey
    - C. Census of Population
    - D. Census of Governments

12. An analyst presented with a set of household records showing age, ethnicity, income, and family status and wishing to study the inter-relationship of all of these variables simultaneously will probably equal
    - A. one four-way cross-tabulation
    - B. four three-way cross-tabulation
    - C. six two-way cross-tabulations
    - D. four single tabulations

3 (#2)

13. Downward communication, from high management to lower levels in an organization, will often not be fully accepted at the lowest levels of an organization unless high-level management
    A. communicates through several levels of mid-level management, where the message can be properly modified and interpreted
    B. communicates directly with the level of the organization it wishes to reach, bypassing any intermediate levels
    C. first establishes an atmosphere in which upward communication is encouraged and listened to
    D. establishes penalties for non-compliance with its communications

13._____

14. A top-level manager sometimes has an inaccurate view of the actual lower-level operations of his agency, particularly of those operations which are not running well.
    Of the following, the MOST frequent cause of this is the
    A. general unconcern of top-level management with the way an agency actually operates
    B. tendency of the people at the lowest level in an agency to lie about their actual performance
    C. unwillingness of top-level management to deal with unfavorable information when it is presented
    D. tendency of mid-level management to edit bad news and unpleasant information from reports directed to top management

14._____

15. In the conduct of productivity analyses, work measurement is a USEFUL technique for
    A. substantiating executive decisions
    B. designing a research study
    C. developing performance yardsticks
    D. preparing a manual of procedure

15._____

16. Issue analysis is closely identified with the "fire-fighting" function of management. As such, issue analysis is a(n)
    A. systematic assessment over time of an agency's strategic options
    B. annual review of the issues that have come up during the past year
    C. basis for a set of procedures to be followed in an emergency
    D. analysis of a specific policy question often performed in a crisis environment

16._____

17. The transportation agency in a large city wishes to study the impact of fare increases on ridership in buses. Ridership data for peak hours has been assembled for the same time period for three geographic subareas (A, B, and C) with approximately the same socio-economic characteristics, residential density, and distance from the central business district (CBD). Subarea A had experienced a moderate fare increase on its bus line; Subarea B had had no fare increase; and Subarea C had experienced a major fare increase during the time period

17._____

In the design of this study, the analysis should be framed:
A. Ridership = f (fare level)
B. Ridership = f (fare level), distance from CBD)
C. Fare level = f (ridership)
D. Ridership = f (fare level, socio-economic characteristics, residential density)

18. What organizational concept is illustrated when a group is organized on an *ad hoc* basis to accomplish a specific goal?
A. Functional Teamwork B. Line/staff
C. Task Force D. Command

18.____

19. The concept of "demand" provides an appropriate theoretical basis for estimating the needs for public services or programs where the service will be on a _____ basis and _____ life-sustaining necessities.
A. fee; involves B. free; involves
C. free; does not involve D. fee; does not involve

19.____

20. Analysts should be wary of relying exclusively on traditional service standards (e.g., one acre of playground per 1,000 population).
Such standards are often DEFICIENT because they tend to overstate
A. the consumer view and understate behavior and values of producers
B. the producer view and understate behavior and values of users or consumers
C. local conditions and understate national conditions
D. behavioral factors and understate practical effects

20.____

21. The BEST measure of the performance of a manpower program would be
A. percentage reduction in unemployment by impacted population groups
B. number of trainees placed in jobs at the beginning of the training program
C. percentage of students completing a training program
D. cost per student of the training program and the job placement effort

21.____

22. Indices are single figures that measure multi-dimensional concepts.
The critical judgment in the construction of an index involves
A. the trade-off between accuracy and simplicity
B. determination of enough data to do the measurement
C. avoidance of all possible error
D. developing a theoretical basis for it

22.____

23. Evaluation of public programs is complicated by the reality that programs tend to reflect negotiated compromises among conflicting objectives.
The absence of clear, unitary objectives PARTICULARLY complicates the
A. assessment of program input or effort
B. development of effectiveness criteria
C. design of new programs to replace the old
D. diagnosis of a program's processes

23.____

5 (#2)

24. The BASIC purpose of the "Super-Agencies" is to   24.____
    A. reduce the number of departments and agencies in the city government
    B. reduce the number of high-level administrators
    C. coordinate agencies reporting to the mayor and supervise agencies in related fields
    D. supervise departments and agencies in unrelated fields

25. In most municipal budgeting systems involving capital and operating budgets, the leasing or renting of facilities is usually shown in   25.____
    A. the operating budget   B. the capital budget
    C. a separate schedule   D. either budget

26. New York City's budgeting procedure is unusual in that budget appropriations are considered in two parts, as follows: 26.____
    A. Capital budget and income budget
    B. Expense budget and income budget
    C. Revenue budget and expense budget
    D. Expense budget and capital budget

27. The "growth rate" referred to in current political and economic discussion refers to change from year to year in a country's   27.____
    A. gross national product   B. population
    C. available labor force   D. capital goods investment

Questions 28-29.

DIRECTIONS: Questions 28 and 29 are to be answered on the basis of the following illustration. Assume that the figures in the chart are cubes.

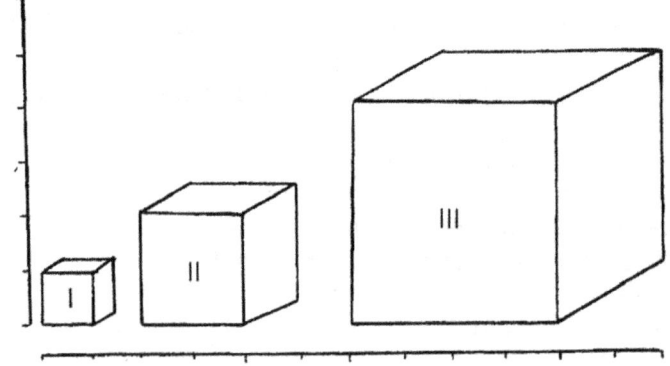

28. In the illustration above, how many times GREATER is the quantity represented by Figure III than the quantity represented by Figure II?   28.____
    A. 2   B. 4   C. 8   D. 16

29. The above illustration illustrates a progression in quantity BEST described as   29.____
    A. arithmetic   B. geometric   C. discrete   D. linear

Questions 30-35.

DIRECTIONS: Questions 30 through 35 are to be answered on the basis of the following chart.

In a national study of poverty trends, the following data have been assembled by interpretation.

Item	Persons Below Poverty, By Residence			
	Number (millions)		Percent	
	U.S.	Metropolitan Areas	U.S.	Metropolitan Areas
2010				
Total	38.8	17.0	22.0	15.3
Under 25 years	20.0	8.8	25.3	18.1
65 years & over	5.5	2.5	35.2	26.9
Black	9.9	5.0	55.1	42.8
Other	28.3	11.8	18.1	12.0
2020				
Total	24.3	12.3	12.2	9.5
Under 25 years	12.2	6.4	13.2	10.4
65 years & over	4.8	2.3	25.3	20.2
Black	7.2	3.9	32.3	24.4
Other	16.7	8.2	9.5	7.3

30. If no other source of data were available, which of the following groups would you expect to have the HIGHEST rate of poverty?
    A. Others over 65
    B. Others under 65
    C. Blacks over 65
    D. Blacks under 65

31. Between 2010 and 2020, the percentage of poor in the United States who were Black
    A. increased from 25.5% to 29.6%
    B. decreased from 55.1% to 32.3%
    C. decreased from 9.9% to 7.2%
    D. stayed the same

32. The data in the second column of the table indicate that, in the metropolitan areas, the number of poor declined by 4.7 million or 36.2% between 2010 and 2020. Yet, the fourth column shows a corresponding decline from 15.3% to 9.5%, or only 5.8%.
    This apparent discrepancy reflects the fact that
    A. metropolitan areas are growing while the number of poor is contracting
    B. two columns in question are based on different sources of information
    C. difference between two percentages is not the same as the percent change in total numbers
    D. tables have inherent errors and must be carefully checked

33. The percentages in each of the last two columns of the table for 2010 and 2020 don't add up to 100%. This is for the reason that
    A. rounding off each entry to the nearest decimal place caused an error in the total such that the total is not equal to 100%
    B. these columns show the percentage of Blacks, aged, etc. who are poor rather than the percentage of poor who are Black, aged, etc.
    C. there was an error in the construction of the table which was not noticed until the table was already in print
    D. there is double counting in the entries in the table; some people ae counted more than once

33.____

34. Data such as that presented in the table on persons below poverty level are shown to a single decimal place because
    A. data in every table should always be shown to a single decimal place
    B. it is the minimal number of decimal places needed to distinguish among table entries
    C. there was no room for more decimal places in the table without crowding
    D. the more accurately a figure is shown the better it is for the user

34.____

35. In comparing the poverty of the young (under 25 years) with that of the older population (65 years and over) in 2010 and 2020, one could REASONABLY conclude that
    A. more young people than old people were poor but older people had a higher rate of poverty
    B. more older people than young people were poor but young people had a higher rate of poverty
    C. there is a greater degree of poverty among the younger population than among the older people

35.____

Questions 36-37.

DIRECTIONS: Questions 36 and 37 are to be answered ONLY on the basis of the information given in the following passage.

Two approaches are available in developing criteria for the evaluation of plans. One approach, designated Approach A, is a review and analysis of characteristics that differentiate successful plans from unsuccessful plans. These criteria are descriptive in nature and serve as a checklist against which the plan under consideration may be judged. These characteristics have been observed by many different students of planning, and there is considerable agreement concerning the characteristics necessary for a plan to be successful.

A second approach to the development of criteria for judging plans, designated Approach B is the determination of the degree to which the plan under consideration is economic. The word "economic" is used here in its broadest sense, i.e., effective in its utilization of resources. In order to determine the economic worth of a plan, it is necessary to use a technique that permits the description of any plan in economic terms and to utilize this technique to the extent that it becomes a "way of thinking" about plans.

36. According to Approach B, the MOST successful plan is generally one which
    A. costs least to implement
    B. gives most value for resources expended
    C. uses the least expensive resources
    D. utilizes the greatest number of resources

36.____

37. According to Approach A, a successful plan is one which is
    A. descriptive in nature
    B. lowest in cost
    C. similar to other successful plans
    D. agreed upon by many students of planning

37.____

Questions 38-40.

DIRECTIONS: Questions 38 through 40 are to be answered ONLY on the basis of the information provided in the following passage.

The primary purpose of control reports is to supply information intended to serve as the basis for corrective action if needed. At the same time, the significance of control reports must be kept in proper perspective. Control reports are only a part of the planning-management information system. Control information includes non-financial as well as financial data that measure performance and isolate variances from standard. Control information also provides feedback so that planning information may be updated and corrected. Whenever possible, control reports should be designed so that they provide feedback for the planning process as well as provide information of immediate value to the control process.

Since the culmination of the control process is the taking of necessary corrective action to bring performance in line with standards, it follows that control information must be directed to the person who is organizationally responsible for taking the required action. Usually the same information, though in a somewhat abbreviated form, is given to the responsible manager's superior. A district sales manager needs a complete daily record of the performance of each of his salesmen; yet, the report forwarded to the regional sales manager summarizes only the performance of each sales district in his region. In preparing reports for higher echelons of management, summary statements and recommendations for action should appear on the first page; substantiating data, usually the information presented to the person directly responsible for the operation, may be include if needed.

38. A control report serves its primary purpose as part of the process which leads DIRECTLY to
    A. better planning for future action
    B. increasing the performance of district salesmen
    C. the establishment of proper performance standards
    D. taking corrective action when performance is poor

38.____

39. The one of the following which would be the BEST description of a control report is that a control report is a form of
    A. planning   B. communication
    C. direction   D. organization

39.____

40. If control reports are to be effective, the one of the following which is LEAST essential to the effectiveness of control reporting is a system of
    A. communication
    B. standards
    C. authority
    D. work simplification

KEY (CORRECT ANSWERS)

1.	A	11.	B	21.	A	31.	B
2.	B	12.	A	22.	A	32.	C
3.	A	13.	C	23.	B	33.	B
4.	B	14.	D	24.	C	34.	D
5.	D	15.	C	25.	A	35.	A
6.	C	16.	D	26.	D	36.	B
7.	D	17.	A	27.	A	37.	C
8.	C	18.	C	28.	C	38.	D
9.	B	19.	D	29.	B	39.	B
10.	D	20.	B	30.	C	40.	D

EXAMINATION SECTION
TEST 1

DIRECTIONS: Each question or incomplete statement is followed by several suggested answers or completions. Select the one that BEST answers the question or completes the statement. *PRINT THE LETTER OF THE CORRECT ANSWER IN THE SPACE AT THE RIGHT.*

1. A percentage of the payment for a contract is held back until the job is completed for one year.
   The MAIN reason for this practice is to insure that the

   A. city doesn't overpay the contractor for the job
   B. contractor will return to correct defective work after the job is completed
   C. contractor will not make unwarranted claims against the city
   D. contractor will pay all his subcontractors

   1._____

2. There are four separate major contracts on a certain building construction project.
   The MAJOR disadvantage of this practice, as compared to the practice of having a single contract, is

   A. the difficulty in coordinating the work
   B. the low level of productivity of the tradesman
   C. cost of the material going into the building is greater
   D. the difficulty in finding competent bidders on the contracts

   2._____

3. Of the following, the PREFERRED way to authorize a contractor to perform work other than required by the contract is by a

   A. T & M order   B. unit price order
   C. lump sum modification   D. change order

   3._____

4. A contract requires that the prime contractor do a certain minimum percentage of the work with his own forces.
   Of the following, the BEST reason for this requirement is to

   A. insure good work
   B. discourage bidders who may not have the ability to do the job
   C. encourage more people to bid the job, thus lowering the bid price
   D. freeze out incompetent subcontractors

   4._____

5. In computing an extra based on the actual cost of work done, the THREE MAJOR items that go into the cost are

   A. taxes, labor, and material
   B. time, taxes, and material
   C. labor, material, and equipment
   D. taxes, labor, and equipment

   5._____

6. A contractor is to be penalized if he exceeds a certain completion date. There is a major strike lasting a month that shuts down all construction.
   Under these conditions, the completion date should be

   6._____

A. held unchanged
B. made two weeks later than the original date
C. made one month later than the original date
D. made six weeks later than the original completion date

7. The one of the following that refers to a Federal safety program in construction is   7.____

   A. OSHA   B. AISC   C. AIEE   D. UL

8. With regard to the placing of concrete, the contractor is GENERALLY   8.____

   A. limited to a specific method by the contract
   B. not permitted to rent equipment to place the concrete
   C. not permitted to pump the concrete into place
   D. permitted to choose his own method of placing the concrete

9. The MOST practical control the inspector or resident engineer has over the contractor when the inspector is not satisfied with the quality of the work is to   9.____

   A. discuss withholding payment on that part of the work that is unsatisfactory
   B. threaten to have the contractor thrown off the job
   C. request that the contractor fire the men responsible for the unsatisfactory work
   D. call the owner of the company and explain the situation to him

10. The MOST practical method of being sure that the architect will be satisfied with the appearance of the exterior brick work for a building is to   10.____

    A. build a sample wall section, for the architect's approval, with the brick that is delivered to the job site
    B. send the architect to the plant supplying the brick to insure that the color and tone of the brick is satisfactory
    C. have the architect's representative on the job while the brick work is being erected to be sure the finished product is satisfactory
    D. put a damage clause in the contract penalizing the contractor if the brick work is not satisfactory to the architect

11. Of the following, the MOST frequent problem that will arise during the construction of a building is   11.____

    A. inability to fit all the reinforcing steel in the space allotted to it
    B. interference in piping and ductwork
    C. inability to keep walls level
    D. settling of the foundation as the load comes on the building

12. To find the number of reinforcing bars that should be in a slab, the inspector SHOULD refer to the   12.____

    A. architect's plan
    B. reinforcing steel design drawings
    C. standard detail drawings
    D. reinforcing steel detail drawings

13. The specifications for a building state that a certain brick type shall be *Stark Brick type XX or equal.*
    The BEST reason for inserting the *or equal* clause is to

    A. permit other companies to compete in supplying the brick
    B. allow other companies to submit their product to determine which is best
    C. limit the suppliers only to those companies whose product is superior to that produced by Stark
    D. allow Stark Brick Company to set the standard for the industry

    13._____

14. In the absence of a formal training program for inspectors, the BEST of the following ways to train a new man who is to do inspection work is to

    A. give him the literature on the subject so that he can learn what he has to know
    B. have him accompany an inspector as the inspector does his work so that he can learn by observing
    C. assign him the job and let him learn on his own
    D. tell him to go to a school at night that specializes in this field so that he will gain the necessary background

    14._____

15. Of the following, the safety practice that is REQUIRED on the construction job site is

    A. safety shoes must be worn by all workers
    B. safety goggles must be worn by all workers
    C. safety helmets must be worn by all workers
    D. all workers must have a safety kit in their possession

    15._____

16. Safety on the job is the concern of

    A. the individual workman only
    B. the contractor only
    C. all parties on the job
    D. the insuring company only

    16._____

17. Frequently, payments due the contractor are delayed many months because of a backlog of work in the agency.
    This practice is considered

    A. *good* because the city saves money by delaying payment
    B. *poor* because the contractors will raise their bids in the future to compensate for the added cost
    C. *poor* because it becomes difficult to compute payments
    D. *good* because it forces the contractor to do good work in order to be sure that he will receive payment

    17._____

18. Provisions are made in a contract for payment for certain items when delivered to the job before installation.
    The MAIN reason for this practice is to

    A. enable better inspection of the items
    B. prevent bottlenecks during construction
    C. give the contractor a quick profit on the items
    D. allow the contractor more time to shop for the items

    18._____

19. The agency that approves payments to building contractors is the 19.____

    A. Corporation Counsel   B. Comptroller's Office
    C. Board of Estimate   D. City Planning Commission

20. The bond that the contractor puts up to insure that he will start work is the 20.____

    A. Bid Bond   B. Payment Bond
    C. Performance Bond   D. Liability Insurance

21. Of the following, the BEST practice to follow in order to minimize claims of damage to 21.____
    adjacent buildings during the construction of a building is to

    A. take out special insurance against such claims
    B. make a detailed survey of the condition of the nearby buildings before construction begins
    C. make a payment to adjacent property owners in advance so that they waive claims of damage to their property
    D. have the buildings underpinned

22. The four MAJOR contracts on a building project are: 22.____

    A. General Construction, Electrical, Plumbing and Drainage, Heating, Ventilating and Air Conditioning
    B. Plumbing, Heating and Ventilating, Air Conditioning, and General Construction
    C. Foundations, Superstructure, Mechanical, and Electrical
    D. Air Conditioning, Electrical, Mechanical, and Structural

23. Oil tanks, when set in place inside a building, are frequently filled with water. 23.____
    The BEST reason for this practice is

    A. to prevent them from floating off their foundation if water fills the room
    B. to enable them to be lifted up more easily
    C. to prevent them from becoming rusted
    D. for emergency use in case of fire

24. The filing system used in the field for correspondence is required to be uniform for all 24.____
    jobs.
    The BEST reason for this requirement is that

    A. there is only one good way of setting up the filing system
    B. the standardized system is compact, thereby saving space
    C. other interested parties such as engineers from the main office will be able to use the files
    D. the contractor's forces will understand the filing system and will be able to extract necessary correspondence

25. Upon excavation to the subgrade of a footing to be placed on piles, the inspector finds 25.____
    that the soil is very poor.
    Of the following, the PROPER action for the inspector to take is to

    A. do nothing
    B. add 20% to the number of piles
    C. notify the engineer's office of this condition
    D. order the contractor to keep excavating until he hits better soil

26. The general contractor is required to submit a progress schedule before starting work. Of the following, the BEST reason for this requirement is to

    A. determine if the contractor intends to complete the job
    B. enable the inspector to determine whether the contractor is on schedule
    C. enable the inspector to estimate monthly payments
    D. check minority hiring

27. If a contractor is falling behind schedule, the FIRST thing to check if the inspector is looking for the cause of this condition is the

    A. number of men he has on the job
    B. efficiency of his crew
    C. availability of equipment needed to do the job
    D. availability of the latest drawings needed by the contractor

28. The critical path method is a method for

    A. finding the best material needed for a specific use
    B. determining the best arrangement of equipment
    C. determining the best time to replace a piece of machinery
    D. scheduling work

29. The contractor states to the inspector that a given structural detail is undersized and unsafe.
    Of the following, the BEST action for the inspector to take in this situation is to

    A. ignore the complaint since the contractor is not an engineer
    B. change the detail by issuing a change order
    C. notify your superiors of the contractor's statements
    D. allow the contractor to modify the detail since it is his responsibility

30. The contractor proposes to use an additive to the concrete to accelerate its set. He asks you, the inspector, for permission to use it.
    Of the following, the FIRST action to take in response to his request is to

    A. check if the use of the additive is permitted by the specifications
    B. tell him to put the request in writing
    C. ask your superior if the use of the additive is acceptable
    D. deny him permission since additives to concrete are not permitted

KEY (CORRECT ANSWERS)

1.	B	16.	C
2.	A	17.	B
3.	D	18.	B
4.	B	19.	B
5.	C	20.	A
6.	C	21.	B
7.	A	22.	A
8.	D	23.	A
9.	A	24.	C
10.	A	25.	A
11.	B	26.	B
12.	D	27.	A
13.	A	28.	D
14.	B	29.	C
15.	C	30.	A

EXAMINATION SECTION
TEST 1

DIRECTIONS: Each question or incomplete statement is followed by several suggested answers or completions. Select the one that BEST answers the question or completes the statement. *PRINT THE LETTER OF THE CORRECT ANSWER IN THE SPACE AT THE RIGHT.*

QUESTIONS 1-16.

Questions 1 to 16, inclusive, refer to the drawings appearing on page 2.

1. The structural support of the flooring is provided by

    A. a concrete slab
    B. timber joists
    C. steel beams
    D. piles

2. The floor area of the plan and conference room measures, most nearly

    A. 18' x 28'
    B. 21' x 30'
    C. 15' x 30'
    D. 17' x 22'

3. The TOTAL number of windows in the building is

    A. 12 B. 11 C. 10 D. 9

4. The CORRECT number of coats of plaster required for this building is

    A. 0 B. 1 C. 2 D. 3

5. The number of doors that measure 2'8" wide is

    A. 1 B. 2 C. 3 D. 4

6. The number of convenience outlets in the superintendent's office is

    A. 0 B. 1 C. 2 D. 3

7. The thickness of the partitions is, in inches, most nearly,

    A. 1 1/2 B. 2 C. 4 D. 6

8. On the plan, just inside the entrance, is a notation 0'-0". This MOST LIKELY represents

    A. the tolerance for the width of the door
    B. the elevation above or below the floor
    C. information relative to the radiator
    D. information relative to the desk

9. The height from floor to ceiling in the superintendent's office is, most nearly,

    A. 8' 0" B. 9' 0" C. 7' 0" D. 8' 6"

10. The height of the tops of the windows from the floor in the inspector's room is, most nearly,

    A. 6' 0" B. 8' 0" C. 7' 6" D. 7' 0"

11. The height of the floor above the ground is, most nearly,

    A. 6' 0" B. 4' 8" C. 3' 4" D. 2' 8"

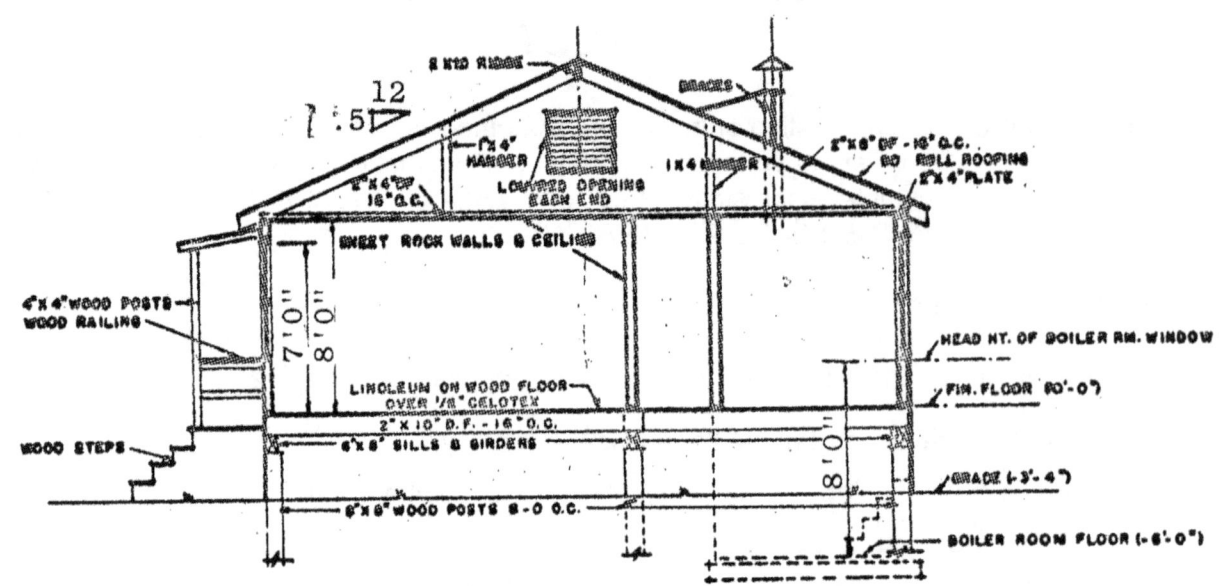

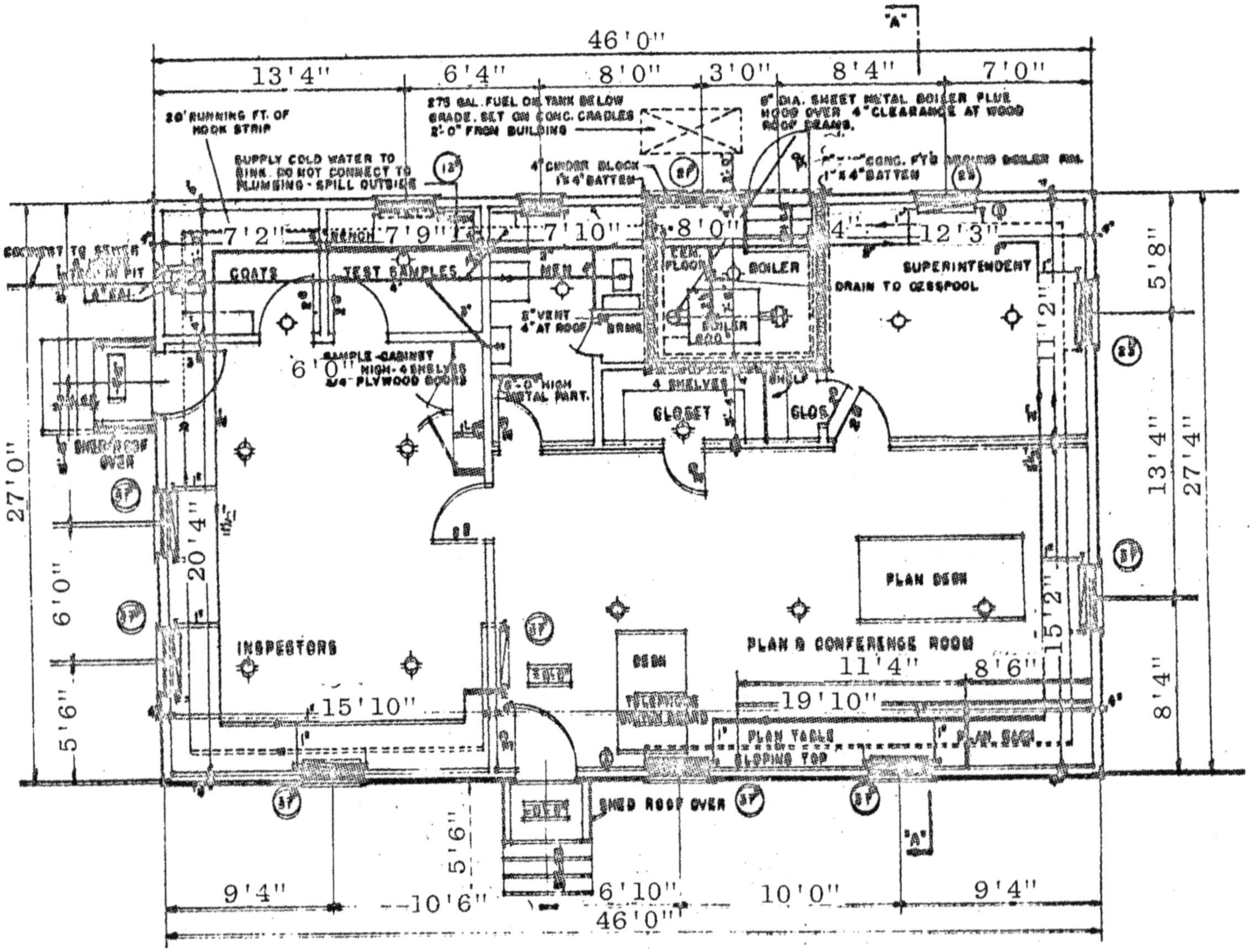

12. Section A-A shows 8" x 8" wood posts supporting the sills and girders. The number of such posts required is, most nearly,

    A. 7 B. 14 C. 21 D. 28

13. Assume the roof rafters extend 1' 0" beyond the outside of the wall. The length of each rafter measures, most nearly,

    A. 14' 8" B. 13' 8" C. 16' 11" D. 15' 11"

14. The wearing surface on the floor is to be

    A. linoleum B. hardwood C. celotex D. asphalt tile

15. Referring to the stairway entrance to the building, if the treads are 10" each, then the distance from the edge of the landing to the entrance measures, most nearly,

    A. 2' 6" B. 3' 0" C. 3' 6" D. 4' 0"

16. From the information shown on the plan and section, the height of each riser in the stairway measures, most nearly,

    A. 10" B. 7 1/2" C. 8" D. 9"

17. The document known as the invitation to bidders does NOT have to include

    A. a description of the job
    B. the location of the job
    C. the plans and specifications for the job
    D. the name and address of the agency to which the bids are to be sent

18. The type of contract generally used on housing or school projects is

    A. unit price   B. cost plus
    C. fixed fee   D. lump sum

19. A lump-sum type of contract may require the contractor to submit a schedule of unit prices. Of the following, the BEST reason for this is that it

    A. prevents the lump sum from being too high
    B. provides a means of making equitable partial payments
    C. enables the estimators to check the total cost
    D. simplifies the selection of the lowest bidder

20. Instructions to bidders for a city housing project may require a bidder to submit a form of non-collusive affidavit.
    The purpose of this is to

    A. bind the contractor to comply with the specifications
    B. obtain an honest bid
    C. make the contractor responsible for collusion with sub-contractors
    D. prevent a contractor from subletting the contract at a lower cost

QUESTIONS 21-23.

The following specification refers to questions 21 to 23, inclusive:
The minimum time of mixing shall be one minute per cubic yard after all the material, including the water, has been placed in the drum, and the drum shall be reversed for an additional two minutes. Mixing water shall be added only in the presence of the inspector.

21. From the above specifications, it is REASONABLE to conclude that

   A. the total mixing time of all the material, including the water, shall be at least 3 minutes for a one-yard batch
   B. the total mixing time of all the material, including the water, shall not be more than 3 minutes
   C. after the material has been mixed for 1 minute, the drum should be discharged and reversed for 2 minutes
   D. the material is mixed for one minute, the water is then added, and mixing continues for 2 more minutes

22. The above specification requires the presence of the inspector at the time the mixing water is added. The PRIMARY reason for this is that he should

   A. see the permit from the water department
   B. obtain the truck number
   C. check the amount of water added
   D. check the quality of water added

23. The above specification MOST LIKELY refers to

   A. transit mix concrete
   B. mortar for brick masonry
   C. plaster for scratch coat
   D. plaster for finish coat

QUESTIONS 24-25.

The following specification applies to questions 24 and 25:
Rough grading shall consist of cutting or filling to the elevation herein established with a permissible tolerance of two inches plus or minus. This tolerance shall be so used that, within any area of 100 feet, it will not be necessary for a later contractor performing fine grading to remove excess or bring additional fill to meet the required elevations.

24. From the above specification, it is REASONABLE to conclude that

   A. the total amount of excavation removed in rough grading should equal the total volume of excavation needed to meet the required elevations
   B. rough grading may end at an elevation 2 inches too high over an area 100' x 100'
   C. rough grading may end at an elevation 2 inches too low over an area 100' x 100'
   D. the contractor performing fine grading will not be permitted to remove excess material

25. Of the following, the BEST reason for specifying the above paragraph is that

   A. a stronger foundation is assured
   B. a savings in concrete will result
   C. by keeping above the water table a dry foundation is assured
   D. it establishes limits for the rough grading contractor

5 (#1)

QUESTIONS 26-28.

The following specification applies to questions 26 to 28 inclusive:

All present walls, cellar floors, foundations, footings, and other existing structural items shall be removed as follows: Within 3 feet of all new building walls, areas and ramp walls, the above work shall be removed to the depth of new construction. Under new footings the above work shall be entirely removed.

26. From the above specification, it is REASONABLE to conclude that   26._____

    A. present walls must be entirely removed if they are located directly under new walls
    B. old footings may be left in place if they are located within three feet of new building walls
    C. an existing foundation must be conpletely removed if located under a new footing
    D. the depth of construction may reach a maximum within 3 feet of new walls

27. The above specification MOST LIKELY refers to removal of   27._____

    A. walls and footings that were located off line
    B. walls and footings located at incorrect grade
    C. walls and footings of demolished buildings
    D. defective foundations as determined by test

28. Of the following titles, the one that is MOST appropriate for the section in which the above specification appears is: 28._____

    A. Work Not in Contract
    B. Removal of City Property
    C. Protection of Excavation
    D. Preparation of Site

QUESTIONS 29-30.

The following specification applies to questions 29 and 30:
All exterior concrete exposed to view and interior walls in rooms to be finished shall be formed of plywood, composition, or steel forms. Finish of remainder may be equivalent to that obtained by use of matched 6-inch roofers.

29. From the above specification, it is REASONABLE to conclude that   29._____

    A. matched 6-inch roofers give a better finish than composition or steel forms
    B. interiors of exterior walls that are to be finished need not be carefully formed
    C. formwork made up of 6-inch roofers may cause honeycombing
    D. exterior concrete exposed to view should be more
    E. carefully formed than other exterior concrete

30. The above specification is MOST LIKELY to be found in a section of the specifications titled: 30._____

    A. Forms and Finish
    B. Exterior Concrete
    C. Unfinished Concrete Surfaces
    D. Reinforcement for Concrete

31. If an acid wash is used on a new concrete surface, it will, MOST LIKELY,

    A. glaze the surface
    B. harden the surface
    C. make the surface soft and spongy
    D. disintegrate the surface

32. Of the following admixtures, the one that is MOST LIKELY to speed the setting of concrete is

    A. lamp black   B. calcium chloride
    C. hydrated lime   D. fly ash

33. The specifications state: Coarse aggregate shall consist of clean hard gravel or crushed stone and shall be graded from 1/8 inch to 3/8 inch with not less than 95% passing a 3/8 inch mesh sieve and not more than 10% passing a No. 8 sieve.
    Of the following, the coarse aggregate that would NOT meet the above specification is:

    A. All of the aggregate is between 1/8 inch and 3/8 inch in size
    B. 50% of the aggregate is 1/8 inch in diameter
    C. 5% of the aggregate is sand
    D. 15% of the aggregate is 1/2 inch in diameter

34. In the concrete for reinforced concrete, coarse agg-regate greater than a specified size is not permitted PRIMARILY because

    A. it is more economical since less water is required in the mix
    B. large sized coarse aggregate may not pass between the reinforced bars
    C. smaller sized coarse aggregate makes a denser concrete
    D. this makes a lighter concrete

35. The specification for formwork for concrete states: Formwork for all slabs shall be set with a camber of 1/4 inch for each 10 ft. of span.
    The BEST reason for this is that the

    A. underside of the finished slab will be level
    B. formwork will have additional strength to resist construction stresses
    C. concrete will flow more easily into the forms
    D. bracing normally required to support the wood formwork will be eliminated

36. Cinder concrete is useful in building construction PRIMARILY because of its

    A. high density   B. imperviousness
    C. frost resistance   D. light weight

37. A tie bar in a cavity wall has a crimp in the center . The purpose of the crimp is to

    A. make the bar more rigid
    B. prevent water from passing across the bar
    C. provide a better bond in the masonry
    D. provide a means of hanging a board to catch surplus mortar

38. Cored brick may sometimes be specified for use as face brick. The minimum thickness between the core and the face of the brick SHALL NOT BE LESS THAN

    A. 1/4"   B. 3/8"   C. 1/2"   D. 3/4"

39. Assume the specifications allow the substitution of sand-lime brick for common brick in certain locations. Of the following, the location at which it is LEAST likely that such substitution would be permitted is

    A. backing-up B. chimney flues
    C. piers   D. walls

40. Of the following, the ONE that may MOST LIKELY be the cause of map cracking in the finish coat of plaster is

    A. a weak brown coat
    B. too much moisture present
    C. a warm dry draft blowing on fresh plaster
    D. too much retarder in the mix

41. An inspector reports a dryout in a room that has just been plastered. The MOST appropriate course of action to take is to

    A. wait until the plaster sets and determine the extent of the damage
    B. order the dryout removed and replastered
    C. order an increase in the amount of retarder used in the mix
    D. allow the contractor to spray water on the dry spot so that setting action may start again

42. The temperature below which it is NOT good practice to do plastering is, in degrees F, most nearly,

    A. 72   B. 65   C. 50   D. 36

43. Gaging plaster that is used to accelerate the setting time of finish coat plaster is, generally,

    A. plaster of Paris   B. hydrated lime
    C. keene's cement   D. dolomitic lime

44. Where bond plaster is specified for the scratch coat, it is generally required that the bond plaster be

    A. mixed with lime putty
    B. mixed neat without the addition of sand
    C. slaked at least 24 hours before use
    D. mixed with gypsum gaging plaster

45. For the finish coat of a three-coat plaster job, it is MOST LIKELY that the specifications would call for

    A. vermiculite   B. silicon
    C. perlite   D. gypsum

46. Good practice in laying asphalt tile requires that the temperature of the room, in degrees F, be NOT LESS THAN

    A. 32 B. 50 C. 70 D. 80

47. The joints in 2" face wood flooring are MOST LIKELY to be

    A. mortise and tenon
    B. tongue and groove
    C. butt
    D. dove-tail

48. Of the following species of wood, the ONE that is MOST LIKELY to be specified for finish flooring in a school or housing project is

    A. Douglas Fir
    B. Sitka Spruce
    C. Northern Hard Maple
    D. Hickory

49. Of the following, the ONE that is MOST LIKELY to be specified for fastening wood flooring in concrete is

    A. dowels in the concrete
    B. sleepers in the concrete
    C. set flooring in fresh concrete
    D. spread thin layer of grout and set flooring therein

50. After asphalt tile is cemented in place, the specifications generally require that it shall be

    A. cleaned only
    B. cleaned and waxed
    C. cleaned and stained
    D. cleaned and shellacked

KEY (CORRECT ANSWERS)

1. B	11. C	21. A	31. D	41. D
2. C	12. C	22. C	32. B	42. C
3. B	13. D	23. A	33. D	43. A
4. A	14. A	24. A	34. B	44. B
5. D	15. B	25. D	35. A	45. D
6. B	16. C	26. C	36. D	46. C
7. C	17. C	27. C	37. B	47. B
8. B	18. D	28. D	38. D	48. C
9. A	19. B	29. D	39. B	49. B
10. D	20. B	30. A	40. A	50. A

EXAMINATION SECTION
TEST 1

DIRECTIONS: Each question or incomplete statement is followed by several suggested answers or completions. Select the one that BEST answers the question or completes the statement. *PRINT THE LETTER OF THE CORRECT ANSWER IN THE SPACE AT THE RIGHT.*

1. One reason for specifying back-puttying in glazed work is that

    A. it seals the window against air and rain leaks
    B. less putty is required in this method
    C. the use of glazing clips is not required
    D. it is easier to apply putty on the inside of the glass than on the outside

2. A specification on finished hardware refers to Roses and Escutcheon plates. These are MOST LIKELY to be installed on

    A. desks   B. blackboards   C. windows   D. doors

3. Of the following statements, the one that MOST CLOSELY identifies the term "house sewer" is: The house sewer is

    A. located outside the building area and connects to the public sewer in the street
    B. located inside the building area and ends at the outside of the front wall of the building
    C. the pipe which carries the discharge from the plumbing fixtures to the house drain
    D. the house drain

4. A concrete level roof is to receive 4-ply composition slag roofing with insulation. The FIRST item to cover the concrete is

    A. the insulation   B. the slag
    C. a layer of felt   D. a bed of hot pitch

5. A common example of a paint thinner is usually

    A. tung oil   B. chinawood oil
    C. lead oxide   D. turpentine

6. In the painting of rooms in a housing project or school by the contractor, the superintendent representing the city is LEAST concerned with

    A. the area covered per man per day
    B. whether the paint is being used at the required spreading rate
    C. the moisture content of the plaster
    D. the condition of the surfaces to be painted

QUESTIONS 7-9.

Questions 7 to 9, inclusive, refer to the diagram shown below:

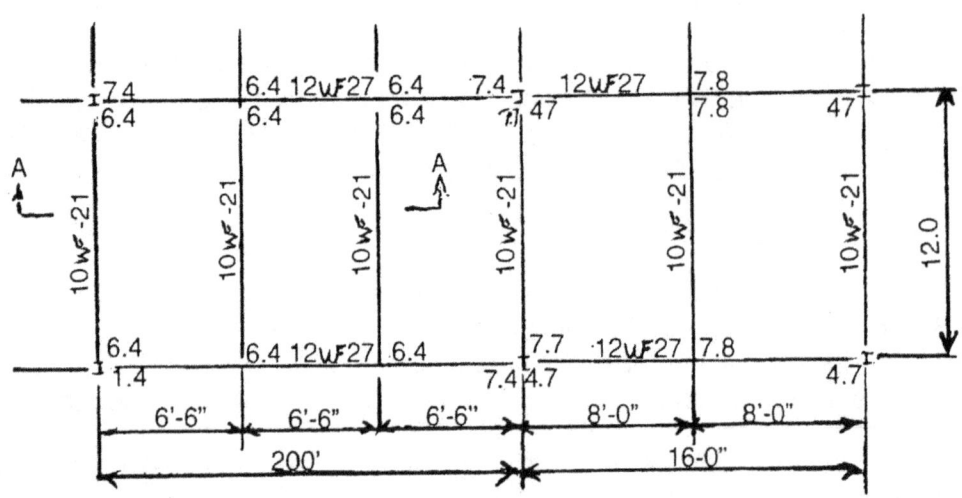

FLOOR PLAN

TOP OF BEAM 3 1/2" BELOW FINISHED FLOOR LEVEL

LIVE LOAD = 100#/SQ.FT.

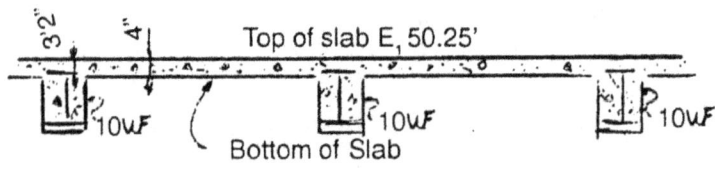

SECTION A-A

7. The elevation of the underside of the 4" slab is most nearly,

   A. 49.92   B. 50.00   C. 50.12   D. 50.25

8. The figures such as 6.4 and 4.7 represent, most nearly, the

   A. deadweight reactions of the slab
   B. distances to the points of 0 shear
   C. maximum moments that the beams carry
   D. end reactions of the beams

9. Of the following, the BEST reason for encasing the steel beams in concrete is to

   A. increase their resistance to corrosion
   B. simplify the formwork
   C. increase the deadweight of the floor
   D. increase their fire resistance

10. Splices in the steel columns of a tall steel frame building are usually located approximately

    A. 2' above the floor
    B. 2' below the floor

C. halfway between floors
D. at the level the floor beams frame into the column

11. Rivets that are to be driven in the field are usually heated until the color is

    A. white   B. light blue   C. cherry red   D. dull black

12. Reinforcing steel is USUALLY bent to its final shape

    A. on the jobsite   B. at the mill
    C. at the warehouse   D. in the shop

13. Copper sheet is USUALLY specified

    A. Birmingham Gage   B. United States Steel Gage
    C. in ounces per square foot   D. in pounds per square yard

14. The thickness of a 16-gage plate is, in inches, most nearly,

    A. 1/16   B. 1/8   C. 3/16   D. 1/4

15. A loose lintel is a lintel that

    A. has less than 4 inches of bearing on the masonry
    B. is not connected to the structural steel work
    C. is used over doors but not over windows
    D. should have a minimum bearing of 8" on the surface on which it rests

16. The diameter of a #6 reinforcing bar is, in inches, most nearly,

    A. 3/8   B. 1/2   C. 5/8   D. 3/4

17. The bent bar marked "A" is USUALLY called a

    A. tylag
    B. government anchor
    C. dead man
    D. strap bar

18. "Legal Curb Level", according to the code, means, most nearly,

    A. the curb level established by the county
    B. the curb level established by the department of public works
    C. that it is 6" above the crown of the road
    D. that it is the elevation established by the law department of the city

19. Of the following soils, the ONE that is MOST compressible is usually

    A. hardpan   B. sand   C. gravel   D. clay

20. The specifications state: Excavated material shall only be considered as rock when the Superintendent agrees that because of its density the most practical and economical method of removing same is by means of explosives. When rock is disintegrated to such an extent that it can readily be loosened by steam shovels or manually by tools not requiring fuel or power, then such material shall be regarded as earth excavation. Referring to the specification above, the MOST NEARLY correct statement is:

    A. A cubic yard boulder is considered rock excavation
    B. Material that can be economically removed only by explosives shall be classified as rock
    C. All disintegrated rock is to be classified under earth excavation
    D. If any material requires a steam shovel for its removal, it shall be classified as rock

21. Of the following, the ONE that is of LEAST importance to the inspector on timber pile driving is the

    A. plumbing of mandrel befroe driving
    B. condition of the pile before driving
    C. plumbness of pile
    D. final position of the pile

22. Of the following, the MOST important advantage in the use of steel shell piles is the

    A. savings in concrete
    B. opportunity for better inspection
    C. simplified pile cap construction
    D. elimination of pile caps

23. The Engineering News-Record formula for piles is $P = \dfrac{2Wh}{s+c}$

    The letter s represents, MOST NEARLY, the

    A. factor of safety used
    B. number of the hammer used
    C. average penetration of the last 5 blows in inches
    D. distance the pile has travelled vertically in feet

24. In the Engineering News-Record formula, the term "Wh" represents, MOST NEARLY, the

    A. weight of pile multiplied by height of hammer falls
    B. bearing energy of the pile
    C. weight of hammer multiplied by the height of fall
    D. speed at which the pile goes inth the ground

25. In the Engineering News-Record formula, the term c represents, MOST NEARLY,

    A. a constant depending upon the type of hammer used
    B. a correction factor that corrects for rebound
    C. the factor that allows a suitable factor of safety
    D. the penetration caused by the last blow

26. If steel weighs 490 #/cu. ft., the weight of a 1-inch square steel bar 1 foot long is, in pounds, *MOST NEARLY*,

   A. .434   B. 3.4   C. 42   D. 49

27. The invert elevation of a sewer is 18.54 at Manhole 1 and 18.22 at Manhole 2, 250 feet from Manhole 1. The slope of the sewer per foot is, *MOST NEARLY*,

   A. .0013   B. .32   C. .01   D. 0.1

QUESTIONS 28-31.
   Questions 28 to 31, inclusive, refer to the diagram shown below.

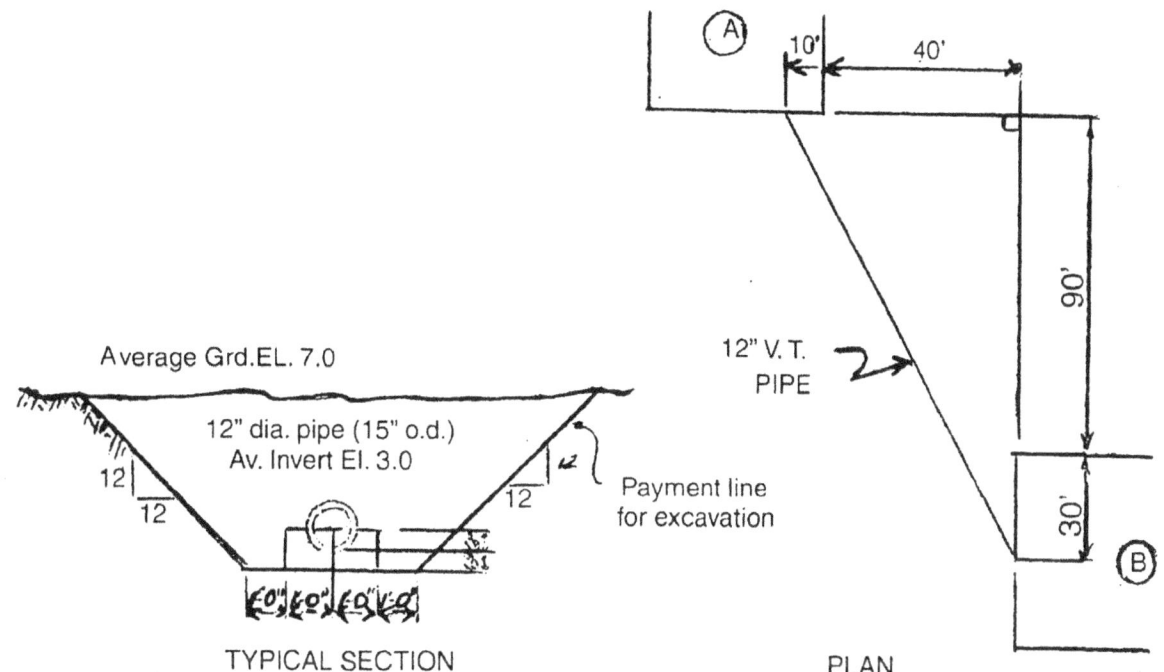

TYPICAL SECTION   PLAN

28. The length of the 12" vitrified pipe between Building A and Building B is, in feet, *MOST NEARLY*,

   A. 120   B. 130   C. 140   D. 150

29. For 100 feet of pipe, the volume of concrete in the concrete cradle under the pipe, is, in cubic yards, *MOST NEARLY*,

   A. 5.0   B. 6.0   C. 7.0   D. 9.0

30. The volume of payment excavation for 100 feet of trench is, in cubic yards, *MOST NEARLY*,

   A. 95   B. 120   C. 140   D. 165

31. The method of excavation shown in the typical section is *USUALLY* called

   A. skeleton sheeted   B. open cut
   C. lined   D. wellpointed

32. Shown below is a section through a concrete retaining wall. The volume of concrete per foot of retaining wall is, in cubic feet, MOST NEARLY,

   A. 23.2
   B. 25.0
   C. 26.8
   D. 28.8

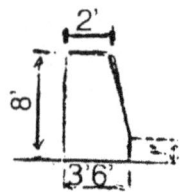

QUESTIONS 33-39.
   Questions 33 to 39, inclusive, refer to the diagram shown below.

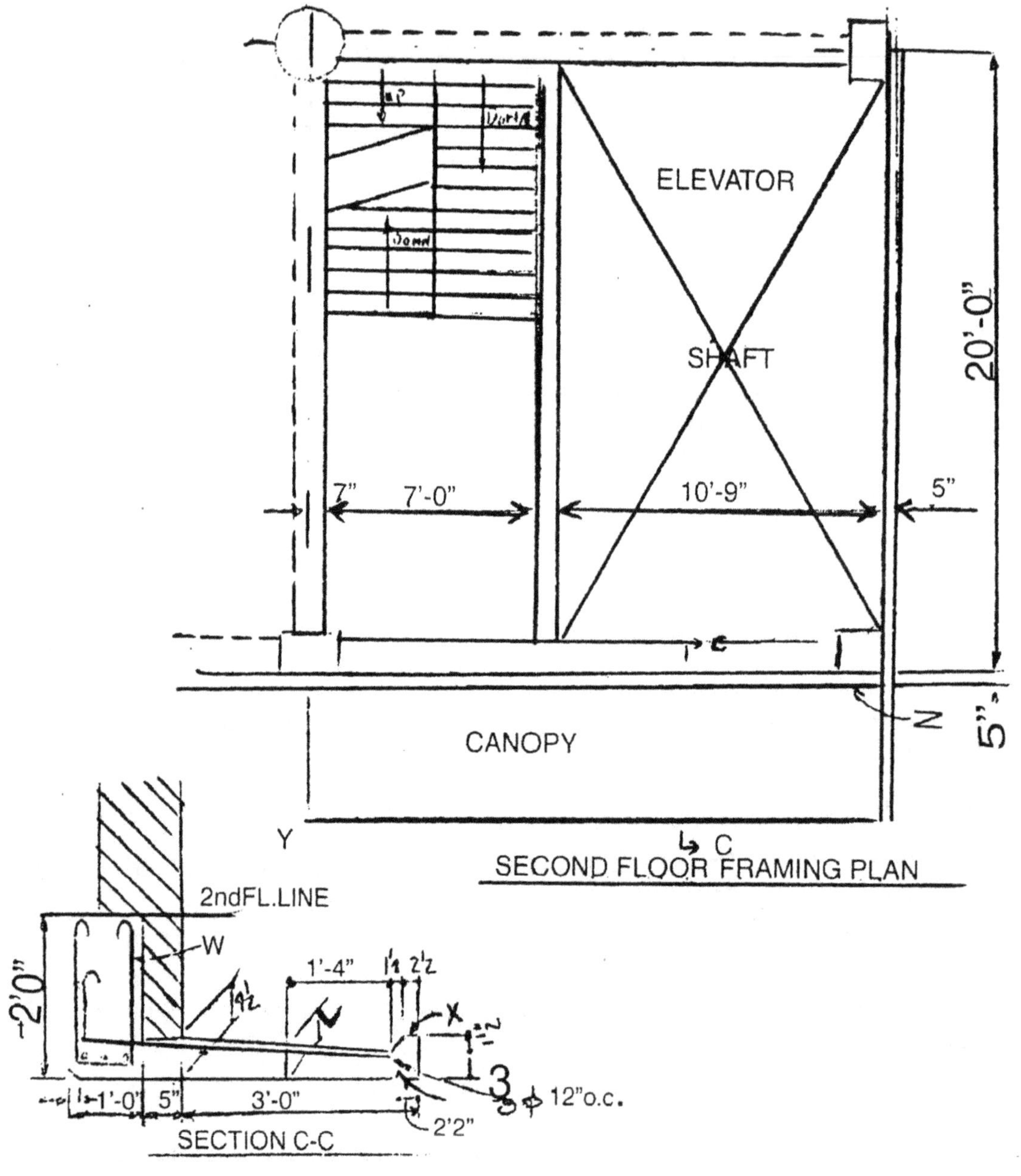

33. The elevation of the top of the outer edge of the canopy marked "X" is, MOST NEARLY,

   A. 20.46   B. 20.42   C. 20.38   D. 20.34

34. The triangular inset on the bottom of the canopy marked "Y" is USUALLY called a   34.____

    A. raggle   B. reglet   C. drip   D. setback

35. Assuming the reinforcing steel is to be stopped 3 inches from the edge of the concrete   35.____
    and the bars marked 3/8" round at 12" o.c. are straight bars, the ordered length of the
    above mentioned bars should be, MOST NEARLY,

    A. 3' 11"   B. 19' 6"   C. 18' 6"   D. 19' 0"

36. In the plan, the line marked "Z" is the   36.____

    A. outside face of the canopy
    B. outside face of the masonry wall
    C. inside face of the reinforced concrete beam
    D. outside face of the reinforced concrete beam

37. The canopy is considered   37.____

    A. pre-stressed concrete
    B. a simply supported beam
    C. a cantilever
    D. pre-cast concrete

38. The bar marked "W" is usually called a   38.____

    A. chair   B. tie bar   C. stirrup   D. spacer

39. The dimension "V" is, in inches, MOST NEARLY,   39.____

    A. 4 1/8   B. 4 1/4   C. 4 3/8   D. 4 1/2

40. Of the following, the BEST way to measure a distance on a map with a scale of 1" =20' is   40.____
    to use a(n)

    A. planimeter set to the correct scale
    B. 50 foot tape
    C. engineer's scale
    D. architect's scale

41. The following appears on a floor plan The   41.____
    3'0" MOST LIKELY represents a

    A. double acting door 3'0" wide
    B. fire door
    C. door, 3'0" wide
    D. masonry opening, 3'0" wide

42. The following symbol on a plumbing plan   42.____
    MOST LIKELY represents a

    A. check valve
    B. vent
    C. sump
    D. trap

43. In the wall section shown below, the dimension that would MOST LIKELY represent the story height is

   A. A
   B. B
   C. C
   D. D

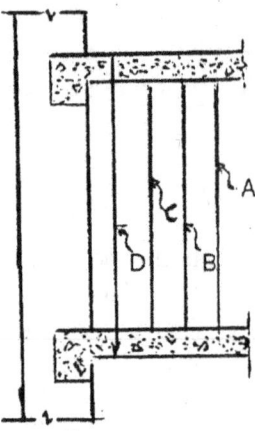

44. According to the section shown in the previous problem, the type of floor construction is, MOST LIKELY,

   A. reinforced concrete
   B. timber joist and wood flooring
   C. steel joist and wood flooring
   D. steel joist and cement flooring

45. A fixed amount of money is held from the contractor for a period of a year after the completion of construction. The BEST reason for this is

   A. that it acts as a security for the repair of defective work after completion of the construction
   B. to penalize the contractor for poor work
   C. the money will be available for modifications in the design of the structure
   D. the money will be available for taxes due

46. A "punch list" is usually a list

   A. showing the checkoff of union dues
   B. showing inspector's attendance
   C. of defects requiring correction by the contractor
   D. of injuries to the contractor's personnel kept for purpose of protecting the city against suit

47. The part of the structure that is MOST LIKELY to be affected by unforeseen existing conditions is the

   A. steel framework   B. plumbing
   C. electrical   D. foundation

48. The specifications state that no live load be placed on a concrete structure immediately following the stripping of its formwork.
The BEST reason for this is

   A. the design of the structure may be wrong
   B. the concrete will not cure properly

C. to allow the easy removal of the formwork
D. to prevent overstressing of the concrete

49. A superintendent should have sufficient confidence in himself and his judgment to take a positive stand when the occasion arises and requires it. A man who changes his mind frequently, reversing his rulings under pressure, does not belong in such a position. However, if he has made a mistake, he should not be obstinate and refuse to alter his position. But too many such mistakes will demonstrate that he is unfit for the job.
From the above statement, it is REASONABLE to conclude that a

   A. superintendent should stick to his decision, right or wrong
   B. good superintendent will never make mistakes
   C. superintendent should not be so bull-headed as to refuse to back down where he is manifestly wrong
   D. man who changes his mind frequently is merely trying to avoid mistakes

50. Assume that a contractor disagrees with a ruling of the general superintendent and you, as a superintendent, believe the contractor is correct. You should

   A. tell him to disregard the ruling until you discuss it with the general superintendent
   B. tell him to stop talking about it since the general superintendent is not going to change his mind
   C. ignore the criticism on the theory that the contractor will oppose any ruling of the general superintendent
   D. tell him you will bring his criticism to the attention of the general superintendent

KEY (CORRECT ANSWERS)

1. A	11. C	21. A	31. B	41. C
2. D	12. A	22. B	32. A	42. D
3. A	13. C	23. C	33. A	43. B
4. D	14. A	24. C	34. C	44. A
5. D	15. B	25. A	35. C	45. A
6. A	16. D	26. B	36. B	46. C
7. A	17. B	27. A	37. C	47. D
8. D	18. A	28. B	38. C	48. D
9. D	19. D	29. A	39. B	49. C
10. A	20. B	30. C	40. C	50. D

EXAMINATION SECTION
TEST 1

DIRECTIONS: Each question or incomplete statement is followed by several suggested answers or completions. Select the one that BEST answers the question or completes the statement. *PRINT THE LETTER OF THE CORRECT ANSWER IN THE SPACE AT THE RIGHT.*

1. Of the following, the BEST reason for using vibrators in concrete construction is to   1.____

    A. remove excess water
    B. consolidate the concrete
    C. increase the slump of the concrete
    D. retard the setting of the concrete

2. When a contractor fails to adhere to an approved progress schedule, he should   2.____

    A. revise the schedule without delay
    B. ask for an extension of time on account of delays
    C. adopt such additional means and methods of construction as will make up for the time lost
    D. take no immediate action with the hope that sufficient time will be available later on that will assure the completion in accordance with the schedule

3. The usual contract for work includes a section entitled *Instructions to Bidders* which states that the   3.____

    A. contractor agrees that he has made his own examination and will make no claim for damages on account of errors or omissions
    B. contractor shall not make claims for damages of any discrepancy, error, or omission in any plans
    C. estimates of quantities and calculations are guaranteed by the board to be correct and are deemed to be a representation of the conditions affecting the work
    D. plans, measurements, dimensions, and conditions under which the work is to be performed are guaranteed by the board

4. Specifications covering brickwork usually require special precautions and protection for work in cold weather.   4.____
   The HIGHEST temperature below which these measures are required is *most nearly*

    A. 50° F   B. 40° F   C. 30° F   D. 20° F

5. Controlled concrete is required for the reinforced concrete frame of a large school building. The ultimate strength of this concrete will be *most nearly* _____ pounds per square inch.   5.____

    A. 1000   B. 3000   C. 5000   D. 7000

6. A lump sum type of contract may require the contractor to submit a schedule of unit prices.   6.____
   The BEST reason for this is that it

    A. prevents the lump sum from being too high
    B. simplifies the selection of the lowest bidder

C. enables the estimators to check the total cost
D. provides a means of making equitable partial payments

7. The concrete test that will BEST determine the consistency of a concrete mix is the

   A. slump test
   B. sieve analysis
   C. calorimetric test
   D. water-cement ratio test

8. The BEST way to evaluate the overall state of completion of a construction project is to check the progress estimate against the

   A. inspection work sheet
   B. construction schedule
   C. inspector's checklist
   D. equipment maintenance schedule

Questions 9-15.

DIRECTIONS: Questions 9 through 15 refer to the sketch below.

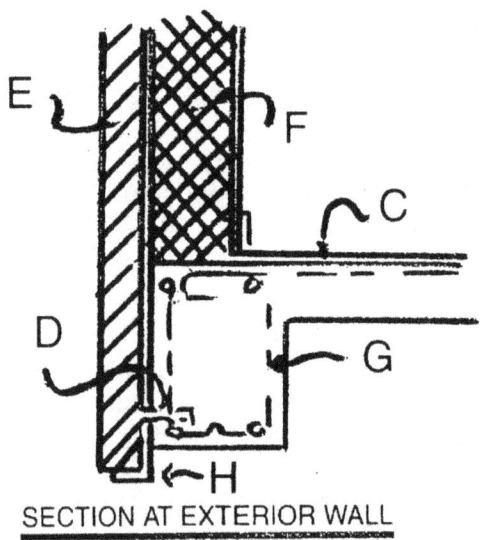

SECTION AT EXTERIOR WALL

9. The floor is made of

   A. air-entrained concrete
   B. reinforced concrete
   C. lightweight concrete
   D. concrete-encased structural steel

10. The exterior wall is a _____ wall.

    A. concrete block
    B. cavity construction
    C. veneer
    D. solid brick

11. Member C is a

    A. deformed bar
    B. hooked bar
    C. plain bar
    D. shear connector

12. Member E is made of

    A. steel   B. wood   C. brick   D. concrete

13. Member F is

    A. concrete block   B. facing brick
    C. glazed tile   D. sheetrock

14. Member G is a

    A. longitudinal bar   B. splice
    C. stirrup   D. tie wire

15. Member H is a

    A. purlin   B. brace   C. guy   D. lintel

16. A projected sash is a(n)

    A. architectural projection from a building exterior which breaks up a smooth pattern of the wall
    B. double-hung window
    C. window that opens inward or outward
    D. window that has a screen attachment

17. In the construction of cellar concrete floors resting on earth, the item that should be checked MOST carefully is that

    A. the earth is wet before pouring
    B. all backfill is granular soil
    C. the earth is dry before pouring
    D. all backfill is properly compacted

18. Specifications state that column dowels are embedded 24 diameters in the footing. The length of embedment for a number 6 bar is _____ inches.

    A. 6   B. 12   C. 18   D. 24

19. After excavating to the subgrade of a footing, an examination of the soil reveals that it is of a poorer quality than the soil in that area and at that elevation shown on the soil borings.
    Of the following types of footings, the one that would be LEAST affected by this condition is a

    A. footing on piles   B. plain concrete footing
    C. combined footing   D. spread footing

20. The MAIN reason for requiring written job reports is to

    A. avoid the necessity of oral orders
    B. develop better methods of doing the work
    C. provide a permanent record of what was done
    D. increase the amount of work that can be done

21. Of the following items, the one which should NOT be included in a proposed work schedule is

    A. a schedule of hourly wage rates and supplementary benefits
    B. an estimated time required for delivery of materials and equipment
    C. the anticipated commencement and completion of the various operations
    D. the sequence and inter-relationship of various operations with those of related contracts

22. A specification requires that brick be laid with *shoved* joints. The BEST reason for this requirement is that it helps the bricklayer to obtain _____ joint(s).

    A. full
    B. plumb vertical
    C. level horizontal
    D. the required thickness of

23. A specification states that access panels to suspended ceilings will be of metal. The MAIN reason for providing access panels is to

    A. improve the insulation of the ceiling
    B. improve the appearance of the ceiling
    C. make it easier to construct the building
    D. make it easier to maintain the building

24. A three-coat plaster job is to be 7/8 inches thick. Of the following, the thickness of the individual coats, in inches, would be *most nearly* scratch

    A. 1/8, brown 1/2, finish 1/4
    B. 3/8, brown 3/8, finish 1/8
    C. 11/16, brown 1/8, finish 1/16
    D. 5/16, brown 1/4, finish 5/16

25. You are assigned to keep a record of the number and volume of all boulders excavated that exceed one cubic yard in volume.
    The MOST probable reason for this order is:

    A. Any delays in excavating due to the boulders may result in a claim
    B. The contractor may receive additional payment for rock excavation
    C. There may be an extra charge for hauling boulders from the jobsite
    D. Excavation where there are large boulders involved is dangerous, and in the event of an accident, you will have appropriate records

KEY (CORRECT ANSWERS)

1. B
2. C
3. A
4. B
5. B

6. D
7. A
8. B
9. B
10. C

11. B
12. C
13. A
14. C
15. D

16. C
17. D
18. C
19. A
20. C

21. A
22. A
23. D
24. B
25. C

TEST 2

DIRECTIONS: Each question or incomplete statement is followed by several suggested answers or completions. Select the one that BEST answers the question or completes the statement. *PRINT THE LETTER OF THE CORRECT ANSWER IN THE SPACE AT THE RIGHT.*

1. Which one of the following is the PRIMARY object in drawing up a set of specifications for materials to be purchased?

   A. Control of quality
   B. Outline of intended use
   C. Establishment of standard sizes
   D. Location and method of inspection

2. In order to avoid disputes over payments for extra work in a contract for construction, the BEST procedure to follow would be to

   A. have contractor submit work progress reports daily
   B. insert a special clause in the contract specifications
   C. have a representative on the job at all times to verify conditions
   D. allocate a certain percentage of the cost of the job to cover such expenses

3. If there is a small amount of water on the surface of a newly-laid concrete sidewalk, the recommended procedure *before* finishing is to

   A. allow it to evaporate
   B. remove it with a broom
   C. sprinkle some dry cement on top
   D. remove it with a float

4. Prior to the installation of equipment called for in the specifications, the contractor is *usually* required to submit for approval

   A. sets of shop drawings
   B. a set of revised specifications
   C. a detailed description of the methods of work to be used
   D. a complete list of skilled and unskilled tradesmen he proposes to use

5. A specification on piles states that plumbness must be within 2% of the pile length. If the pile length is 30 feet, the MAXIMUM amount that the pile may be out of plumb is, in inches, *most nearly*

   A. 5   B. 6   C. 7   D. 8

6. The number of days that it will take high early strength concrete to equal the 28-day strength of normal portland cement concrete is *most nearly*

   A. 1   B. 3   C. 7   D. 12

7. Specifications may state that a standpipe system will be provided in each building. The MAIN purpose of a standpipe system is to

   A. supply the roof water tank
   B. provide water for firefighting

C. circulate water for the heating system
D. provide adequate pressure for the water supply

8. The drawing which should be used as a legal reference when checking completed construction work is the _____ drawing.

   A. contract
   B. assembly
   C. working or shop
   D. preliminary

9. Efflorescence may BEST be removed from brickwork by washing with a solution of _____ acid.

   A. muriatic   B. citric   C. carbonic   D. nitric

10. The MAIN difference between sheet glass and plate glass is

    A. the surface finish of the two types of glass
    B. the heat absorbing qualities of the two types of glass
    C. plate glass is thinner than sheet glass
    D. plate glass is tempered while sheet glass is not tempered

11. Construction joints in the concrete columns of a multistory building are *usually* located

    A. at floor level
    B. 1 foot above floor level
    C. at the underside of floor slab
    D. at the underside of deepest beam framing into the column

12. A contractor on a large construction project *usually* receives partial payments based on

    A. estimates of completed work
    B. actual cost of materials delivered and work completed
    C. estimates of material delivered and not paid for by the contractor
    D. the breakdown estimate submitted after the contract was signed and prorated over the estimated duration of the contract

13. According to the building code, masonry footings shall extend at least 4' below finished grade.
    The PRIMARY reason for this is to

    A. get below the frost line
    B. make the foundation stronger
    C. keep water out of the basement
    D. reach a lower soil strata where better bearing material can be found

14. Good inspection methods require that the inspector

    A. be observant and check all details
    B. constantly check with the engineer who designed the school
    C. apply specifications according to his interpretation
    D. permit slight job variation to establish good public relations

Questions 15-19.

DIRECTIONS: Questions 15 through 19 refer to the following specification for wood flooring. In answering these questions, refer to this specification.

2" x 4" wood sleepers laid flat @ 16" o.c.
1" x 6" sub flooring, laid diagonally; cut at butt joints with parallel cuts; joints at center of sleepers, well staggered, no two joints side by side. Not less than 1/8" space between boards.
One layer of 15# asphalt felt on top of sub-floor.
Finish floor - North Rock Maple, T & G, laid perpendicular to sleepers; 8d nails not more than 12" apart; end joints well scattered with at least 2 flooring strips between joints.
Flooring 25/32" x 2 1/4" face - 1st quality.

15. It is *most likely* that the floor referred to in the specification is to be laid

    A. directly on the ground
    B. on a concrete base
    C. on wood joists
    D. on steel beams

16. The BEST reason for specifying that the sub-flooring be parallel cut at butt joints is that this

    A. requires less material
    B. provides staggered joints
    C. provides more nailing surface
    D. allows the joint to fall between sleepers

17. The BEST reason for specifying a minimum space between the sub-floor boards is that it

    A. saves on material
    B. reduces creaking
    C. allows for expansion
    D. prevents dry rot

18. The BEST reason for specifying at least 2 flooring strips between joints in the finish flooring is that

    A. it looks better
    B. it is more economical
    C. each board is supported by two adjoining boards
    D. each finish board is supported by at least two sub-floor boards

19. The BEST reason for placing asphalt felt on top of the sub-floor is to

    A. deaden noise
    B. preserve the wood
    C. reduce dampness
    D. permit movement

20. Assume you are recommending in a report to your superior that a radical change in a standard maintenance procedure should be adopted.
    Of the following, the MOST important information to be included in this report is

    A. a list of the reasons for making this change
    B. the names of the other GSSM who favor the change
    C. a complete description of the present procedure
    D. amount of training time needed for the new procedure

21. Specifications require that the first floor beams of a building must be in place before backfill is placed against the foundation walls.
    The BEST reason for this requirement is that

    A. without the first floor beams in place, the wall may become overstressed
    B. it is easier to inspect the first floor construction when the backfill is not in place
    C. the utilities up to the first floor level should be in place before backfill is placed
    D. the boiler setting hung from the first floor must be in place before backfill is placed

22. The frequency with which job reports are submitted should depend MAINLY on

    A. how comprehensive the report has to be
    B. the amount of information in the report
    C. the availability of an experienced man to write the report
    D. the importance of changes in the information included in the report

23. Assume that a contractor proposed to start the roofing three days after pouring the concrete roof slab.
    This proposal is

    A. *good,* mainly since it will speed the construction
    B. *good,* mainly since it will assist in curing the concrete
    C. *poor* in cold weather but is all right in warm weather
    D. *poor,* mainly since excess water in the concrete may bulge the roofing

24. In performing field inspectional work, an inspector is the contact man between the public and the board, and it is his job to secure compliance through the maximum utilization of persuasion and education and the minimum application of coercion.
    According to the above statement, an inspector performing inspectional duties should

    A. seek to obtain voluntary compliance and use coercion only as a last resort
    B. be conciliatory on all issues of non-compliance and not take an attitude of firmness and authority
    C. maintain a strictly impersonal attitude in the exercise of his duties at all times
    D. use the threat of legal action to secure conformance with specified requirements

25. A specification requires that brick should be thoroughly wet before using.
    Of the following, the BEST reason for this requirement is that

    A. wetting the brick uncovers hidden flaws
    B. it is easier to shove wet brick into place
    C. wetting cleans the pores of the brick ensuring a stronger bond
    D. wetting decreases absorption of water from the mortar

KEY (CORRECT ANSWERS)

1.	A	11.	A
2.	C	12.	A
3.	A	13.	A
4.	A	14.	A
5.	C	15.	B
6.	C	16.	C
7.	B	17.	C
8.	A	18.	C
9.	A	19.	C
10.	A	20.	A

21. A
22. D
23. D
24. A
25. D

TEST 3

DIRECTIONS: Each question or incomplete statement is followed by several suggested answers or completions. Select the one that BEST answers the question or completes the statement. *PRINT THE LETTER OF THE CORRECT ANSWER IN THE SPACE AT THE RIGHT.*

Questions 1-4.

DIRECTIONS: Questions 1 to 4 refer to the sketch below.

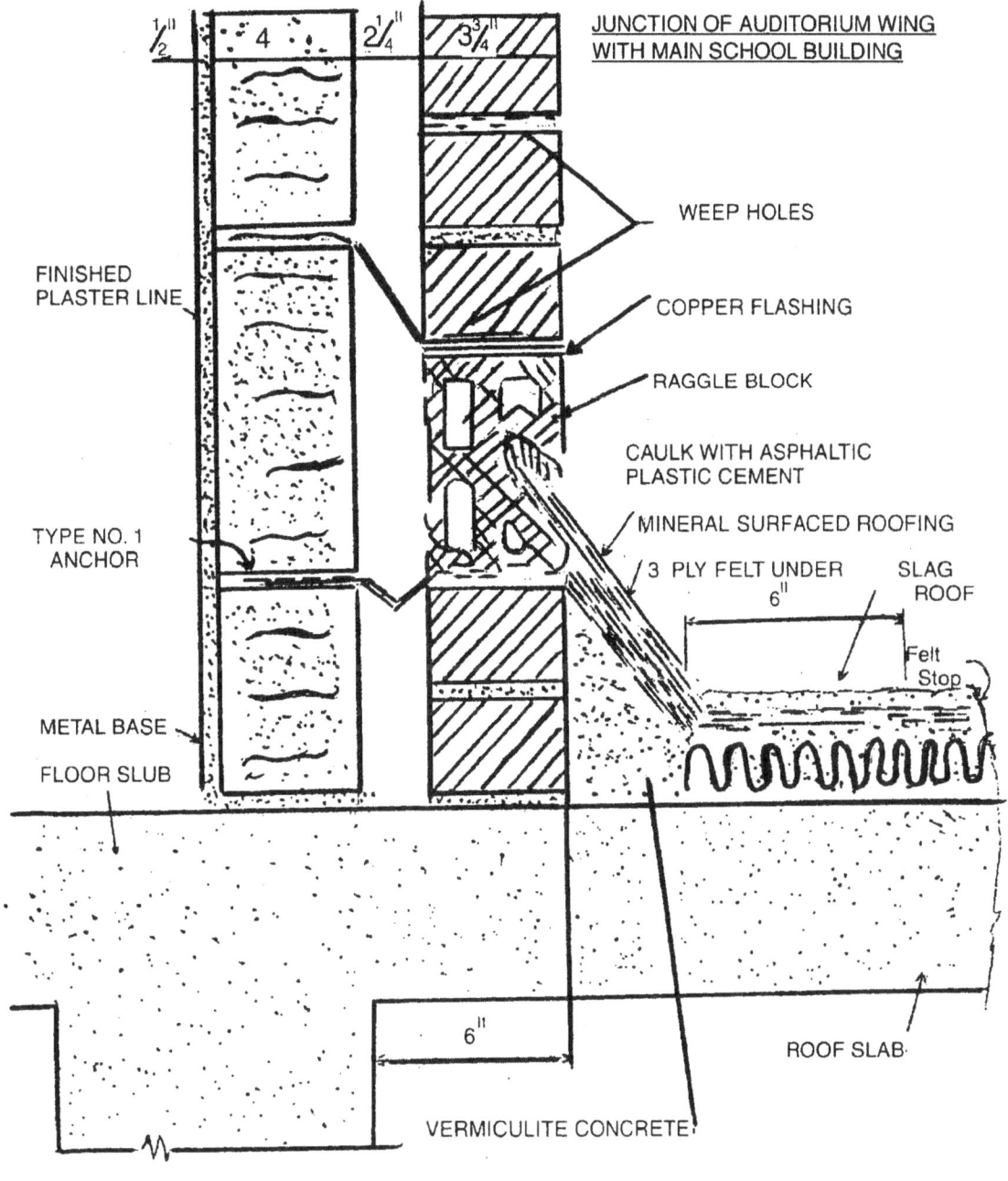

1. The 1/2" of plaster would *most likely* be applied in _____ coats. 1.____

  A. one B. two C. three D. four

2. Vermiculite concrete is PRIMARILY _____ concrete.

   A. low-slump
   B. water-resistant
   C. an air-entrained
   D. a lightweight

3. Which of the following statements relating to copper flashing is CORRECT? It

   A. is perforated in the air space
   B. consists of one solid continuous sheet
   C. consists of 2-inch strips spaced every foot
   D. is provided to prevent the fall of mortar into the air space

4. The 4-inch thick material is *most likely*

   A. cinder block
   B. gypsum block
   C. brick
   D. terra cotta

5. A rowlock course of brick is one in which the bricks are laid

   A. on their 2 1/4" x 8" surface
   B. in an interlocking fashion
   C. with dowels at set intervals
   D. in a one-header followed by a one-stretcher course

6. Specifications for excavation for spread footings require that machine excavation be to within a foot of the final subgrade and the remainder of the excavation shall be by hand. The BEST reason for this requirement is to

   A. prevent cave-ins near the excavation
   B. cut down on the amount of fill needed
   C. prevent excavation below the subgrade
   D. insure that the area in the vicinity of the footing not be excessively disturbed

7. The CHIEF purpose in preparing an outline for a report is *usually* to insure that

   A. the report will be grammatically correct
   B. every point will be given equal emphasis
   C. principal and secondary points will be properly integrated
   D. the language of the report will be of the same level and include the same technical terms

8. One of the properties of tempered plate glass which affects installation is that it

   A. has a blue tinge
   B. cannot be cut after the glass is tempered
   C. does not bond with putty or glazing compound
   D. cracks more easily than ordinary plate glass

9. In assigning the men to various jobs, the BEST principle for a supervisor to follow is to

   A. study the men's abilities and assign them accordingly
   B. rotate a man from job to job until you find one which he can do well
   C. assign each of them to a job and let them adjust to it in their own way
   D. assume that men appointed to the position can do all parts of the work equally well

10. With respect to waterproofing existing basements, the MOST effective and lasting repairs are those made

   A. on the earth side of a basement wall
   B. on the inside basement wall surface
   C. on the floor
   D. in the mortar joints

11. During the actual construction work, the CHIEF value of a construction schedule is to

   A. insure that the work will be done on time
   B. reveal when production is behind schedule
   C. show how much equipment and material is required for the project
   D. furnish data as to the methods and techniques of construction operations

12. When building the formwork for a 12" doubly reinforced concrete wall, the USUAL order of construction is place the

   A. formwork for both faces of the wall; then place the reinforcing steel
   B. reinforcing steel and then place the formwork for both faces of the wall
   C. formwork for one face of the wall, place the reinforcing steel, and then place the formwork for the other face of the wall
   D. formwork for one face of the wall, place the reinforcing steel for one face, place the formwork for the other face of the wall, and then place the reinforcement for the second face

13. The GREATEST period of time must elapse between

   A. pouring and stripping concrete formwork
   B. placing reinforcing steel and pouring concrete
   C. applying the finish plaster coat and painting a plastered wall
   D. applying the first and second coats of a 3-coat plaster job for a wall

14. A fixed amount of money is generally withheld from the contractor for a definite period after the completion of construction.
The BEST reason for this is

   A. that the money will be available for taxes due
   B. to penalize the contractor for poor work
   C. that it is a security for the repair of any defective work
   D. that the money will be available for modifications in the design of the structure

15. The practice of applying the brown coat to a wall on the day after the scratch coat of gypsum plaster was applied is GENERALLY considered

   A. satisfactory
   B. satisfactory only if the temperature is between 50° and 70° F
   C. unsatisfactory because 7 days must elapse between the application of the scratch and brown coats
   D. unsatisfactory because at least 3 days must elapse between the application of the scratch and brown coats

16. Fiberboard material 2 inches thick is placed on a flat reinforced concrete roof. The PRIMARY function of this 2 inch thick material is to

    A. act as a vapor barrier
    B. soundproof the rooms below
    C. prevent loss of heat from the building
    D. keep water from penetrating the ceiling below

17. The PRIMARY purpose of adding lime to a mortar mix is to

    A. improve the appearance of the mortar
    B. increase the workability of the mortar
    C. increase the strength of the mortar
    D. improve the bearing capacity of the wall

18. Assume that excavation is taking place adjacent to a building on a spread footing and a building on pile foundations.
    Extreme care must be exercised in excavating

    A. near the pile-supported building because the soil in the area is of poor quality
    B. near a building on spread footings because the concrete footings may crack
    C. for a pile-supported foundation because heavy loads are involved
    D. near a building on spread footings because of the danger of undermining the foundations

19. An inspector inspecting a large building under construction inspected brickwork at 9 M., formwork at 10 A.M., and concrete at 11 A.M. and did his office work in the afternoon. He followed the same pattern daily for months.
    This procedure is

    A. *bad* because not enough time is devoted to concrete work
    B. *bad* because the tradesmen know when the inspections will occur
    C. *good* because it is methodical and he does not miss any of the trades
    D. *good* because it gives equal amount of time to the important trades

20. If a supervisor finds a discrepancy between the plans and specifications, he should

    A. always follow the plans
    B. ask for an interpretation
    C. always follow the specifications
    D. follow the plans if the difference is in dimensions

KEY (CORRECT ANSWERS)

1.	B	11.	B
2.	D	12.	C
3.	B	13.	C
4.	A	14.	C
5.	A	15.	A
6.	D	16.	C
7.	C	17.	B
8.	B	18.	D
9.	A	19.	B
10.	A	20.	B

EXAMINATION SECTION
TEST 1

DIRECTIONS: Each question or incomplete statement is followed by several suggested answers or completions. Select the one that BEST answers the question or completes the statement. *PRINT THE LETTER OF THE CORRECT ANSWER IN THE SPACE AT THE RIGHT.*

1. The specification states: *The value of each change order shall be computed separately by cost of labor and materials, plus equipment allowance, plus overhead and profit.* The MOST probable value of overhead and profit is _____% of the cost of labor and materials plus equipment allowance.

   A. 5   B. 15   C. 34   D. 55

   1._____

2. In the specifications is an item: *Equipment Allowance: Shall include rental of necessary equipment plus 9% of this rental.*
   According to the above specification, if a piece of equipment rents for $35 per day, Equipment Allowance for this equipment rented for 11 days is MOST NEARLY

   A. $484.00   B. $378.42   C. $385.00   D. $419.65

   2._____

3. A supplier quotes a list price of $172.00 less 15 and 10 percent for twelve tools. The ACTUAL cost for these twelve tools is MOST NEARLY

   A. $146   B. $132   C. $129   D. $112

   3._____

4. Which one of the following is the PRIMARY object in drawing up a set of specifications for materials to be purchased?

   A. Control of quality
   B. Outline of intended use
   C. Establishment of standard sizes
   D. Location and method of inspection

   4._____

5. In order to avoid disputes over payments for extra work in a contract for construction, the BEST procedure to follow would be to

   A. have contractor submit work progress reports daily
   B. insert a special clause in the contract specifications
   C. have a representative on the job at all times to verify conditions
   D. allocate a certain percentage of the cost of the job to cover such expenses

   5._____

6. You wish to order sponges in the most economical manner. Keeping in mind that large sponges can be cut up into many smaller sizes, the one of the following that has the LEAST cost per cubic inch of sponge is _____ sponges @ _____.

   A. 2" x 4" x 6"; $.24
   B. 4" x 8" x 12"; $1.44
   C. 4" x 6" x 36"; $4.80
   D. 6" x 8" x 32"; $9.60

   6._____

7. The cost of a certain job is broken down as follows:
   Materials $375
   Rental of equipment 120
   Labor   315
   The percentage of the total cost of the job that can be charged to materials is MOST NEARLY _____%.

   A. 40   B. 42   C. 44   D. 46

8. Partial payments to outside contractors are USUALLY based on the

   A. breakdown estimate submitted after the contract was signed
   B. actual cost of labor and material plus overhead and profit
   C. estimate of work completed which is generally submitted periodically
   D. estimate of material delivered to the job

9. Building contracts usually require that estimates for changes made in the field be submitted for approval before the work can start.
   The MAIN reason for this requirement is to

   A. make sure that the contractor understands the change
   B. discourage such changes
   C. keep the contractor honest
   D. enable the department to control its expenses

10. If the cost of a broom went up from $4.00 to $6.00, the percent INCREASE in the original cost is

    A. 20   B. 25   C. 33 1/3   D. 50

11. The AVERAGE of the numbers 3, 5, 7, 8, 12 is

    A. 5   B. 6   C. 7   D. 8

12. The cost of 100 bags of cotton cleaning cloths, 89 pounds per bag, at 7 cents per pound is

    A. $549.35   B. $623.00   C. $700.00   D. $890.00

13. If 5 1/2 bags of sweeping compound cost $55,00, then 6 1/2 bags would cost

    A. $60.00   B. $62.50   C. $65.00   D. $67.00

14. The cost of cleaning supplies in a project averaged $330.00 a month during the first 8 months of the year.
    How much can be spent each month for the last four months if the total amount that can be spent for cleaning supplies for the year is $3,880?

    A. $124   B. $220   C. $310   D. $330

15. The cost of rawl plugs is $2.75 per gross. The cost of 2,448 rawl plugs is

    A. $46.75   B. $47.25   C. $47.75   D. $48.25

16. A caretaker received $70.00 for having worked from Monday through Friday, 9 A.M. to 5 P.M. with one hour a day for lunch.
The number of hours the caretaker would have to work to earn $12.00 is

A. 10
B. 6
C. 70 divided by 12
D. 70 minus 12

17. Assume that an employee is paid at the rate of $5.43 per hour with time and a half for overtime past 40 hours in a week.
If he works 43 hours in a week, his gross weekly pay is

A. $217.20
B. $219.20
C. $229.59
D. $241.64

18. Kerosene costs 36 cents a quart.
At that rate, two gallons would cost

A. $1.44
B. $2.16
C. $2.88
D. $3.60

Questions 19-21.

DIRECTIONS: Questions 19 through 21 are to be answered on the basis of the following table.

	Man Days Borough 1		Man Days Borough 2		Man Days Borough 3		Man Days Borough 4	
	Oct.	Nov.	Oct.	Nov.	Oct.	Nov.	Oct.	Nov.
Carpenter	70	100	35	180	145	205	120	85
Plumber	95	135	195	100	70	130	135	80
House Painter	90	90	120	80	85	85	95	195
Electrician	120	110	135	155	120	95	70	205
Blacksmith	125	145	60	180	205	145	80	125

19. In accordance with the above table, if the average daily pay of the five trades listed above is $47.50, the approximate labor cost of work done by the five trades during the month of October for Borough 1 is MOST NEARLY

A. $22,800
B. $23,450
C. $23,750
D. $26,125

20. In accordance with the above table, the Borough which MOST NEARLY made up 22.4% of the total plumbing work force for the month of November is Borough

A. 1
B. 2
C. 3
D. 4

21. In accordance with the above table, the average man days per month per Borough spent on electrical work for all Boroughs combined is MOST NEARLY

A. 120
B. 126
C. 130
D. 136

22. When preparing an estimate for a certain repair job, you determine that $125 worth of materials and 220 man-hours are required to complete the job.
If your man-hour cost is $5.25 per hour, the TOTAL cost of this repair job is

A. $1,030
B. $1,155
C. $1,280
D. $1,405

23. Assume that in determining the total cost of a repair job, a 15% shop cost is to be added to the costs of material and labor.
    For a repair job which cost $200 in materials and $600 in labor, the shop cost is

    A. $30   B. $60   C. $90   D. $120

24. Assume that in quantity purchases, the city receives a discount of 33 1/3%.
    If a one gallon can of paint retails at $5.33 per gallon, the cost of 375 gallons of this paint is MOST NEARLY

    A. $1,332.50   B. $1,332.75   C. $1,333.00   D. $1,333.25

25. Assume that eight barrels of cement together weigh a total of 3004 lbs. and 12 oz.
    If there are four bags of cement per barrel, then the weight of one bag of cement is HOST NEARLY _____ lbs.

    A. 93.1   B. 93.5   C. 93.9   D. 94.3

26. Lumber is usually sold by the board foot, and a board foot is defined as a board one foot square and one inch thick.
    If the price of one board foot of lumber is 18 cents and you need 20 feet of lumber 6 inches wide and 1 inch thick, the cost of the 20 feet of lumber is

    A. $1.80   B. $2.40   C. $3.60   D. $4.80

27. Assume that a trench is 42" wide, 5' deep, and 100' long. If the unit price of excavating the trench is $35 per cubic yard, the cost of excavating the trench is MOST NEARLY

    A. $2,275   B. $5,110   C. $7,000   D. $21,000

28. No single activity has a very large effect on the final price of the complete housing structure and, therefore, the total cost is not affected appreciably by the price policy of any component.
    From the above statement, you may conclude that

    A. we cannot hope for substantial reductions in housing costs
    B. the builder must assume responsibility for the high cost of construction
    C. a 10% reduction in the cost of materials would result in much less than a 10% reduction in the cost of housing
    D. federal government financing would reduce the city's cost of public housing

29. Four board feet of lumber, listed at $350 per M, will cost

    A. $3.50   B. $1.40   C. $1.80   D. $4.00

30. The cost of material is approximately 3/8ths of the total cost of a certain job.
    If the total cost of the job is $127.56, then the cost of material is MOST NEARLY

    A. $47.83   B. $48.24   C. $48.65   D. $49.06

31. It takes four men six days to do a certain job. Working at the same speed, the number of days it will take three men to do this job is

    A. 7   B. 8   C. 9   D. 10

32. A contractor on a large construction project USUALLY receives partial payments based on 32._____

    A. estimates of completed work
    B. actual cost of materials delivered and work completed
    C. estimates of material delivered and not paid for by the contractor
    D. the breakdown estimate submitted after the contract was signed and prorated over the estimated duration of the contract

33. In estimating the cost of a reinforced concrete structure, the contractor would be LEAST concerned with 33._____

    A. volume of concrete
    B. surface area of forms
    C. pounds of reinforcing steel
    D. type of coarse aggregate

34. Assume that an employee is paid at the rate of $6.25 per hour with time and a half for overtime past 40 hours in a week. 34._____
    If she works 45 hours in a week, her gross weekly pay is

    A. $285.49   B. $296.88   C. $301.44   D. $325.49

35. Cleaning fluid costs $1.19 a quart. 35._____
    If there is a 10% discount for purchases over 5 gallons, how much will 8 gallons cost?

    A. $34.28   B. $38.08   C. $42.28   D. $43.43

KEY (CORRECT ANSWERS)

1. B	11. C	26. A
2. D	12. B	27. A
3. B	13. C	28. C
4. A	14. C	29. B
5. C	15. A	30. A
6. B	16. B	31. B
7. D	17. D	32. A
8. C	18. C	33. D
9. D	19. C	34. B
10. D	20. B	35. A
	21. B	
	22. C	
	23. D	
	24. A	
	25. C	

TEST 2

DIRECTIONS: Each question or incomplete statement is followed by several suggested answers or completions. Select the one that BEST answers the question or completes the statement. *PRINT THE LETTER OF THE CORRECT ANSWER IN THE SPACE AT THE RIGHT.*

1. When windows are mounted side by side, the vertical piece between them is called the

    A. muntin B. casement C. sash D. mullion

2. Approximately how many pounds of 16d nails would be required for 1,000 square feet of floor framing area?

    A. 4-5 B. 7-8 C. 8-10 D. 10-12

3. What is represented by the electrical symbol shown at the right?

    A. Transformer B. Buzzer
    C. Telephone D. Bell

4. Which of the following structures would typically require a relatively higher grade of lumber?

    A. Vertical stud B. Joist
    C. Column D. Mud sill

5. A dump truck with a capacity of 10-12 cubic yards must load, drive, dump, and reposition itself over a 1-mile haul distance.
   What average amount of time should be estimated for this sequence?

    A. 15 minutes B. 30 minutes
    C. 1 hour D. 2 hours

6. The stripping of forms that are to be reused should be charged as

    A. common labor B. masonry labor
    C. carpentry labor D. material credit

7. What type of brick masonry unit is represented by the drawing shown at the right?
    A. Modular
    B. Norwegian
    C. 3 core
    D. Economy

8. Which of the following would be a typical thickness of a crushed-rock base course for an area of asphalt paving?

    A. 2" B. 5" C. 7" D. 10"

9. Which of the following wood floor materials would be MOST expensive to install?   9._____

   A. Unfinished plank   B. Walnut parquet
   C. Maple strip   D. Oak parquet

10. When calculating the air-conditioning needs for a building, a loss factor of _____ should   10._____
    be used for the exposure of walls to common heated surfaces.

    A. 2.0   B. 3.5   C. 6.0   D. 7.5

11. Approximately how many linear feet of moldings, door and window trim, handrails, or   11._____
    similar parts can a carpenter install in a typical work day?

    A. 100   B. 250   C. 400   D. 500

12. Which of the following constructions is NOT typically found in bathroom lavatories?   12._____

    A. Enameled pressed steel   B. Cast iron
    C. Cast ceramic   D. Stainless steel

13. What size reinforcing bar is typically used for masonry walls?   13._____

    A. 3   B. 4   C. 7   D. 9

14. Which of the following would NOT be a typical source for a cost-per-square-foot esti-   14._____
    mate?

    A. Architect   B. Engineer
    C. Appraiser   D. Building contractor

15. Approximately how many stair treads with risers can a carpenter install in an average   15._____
    work day?

    A. 5-8   B. 10-12   C. 15-18   D. 21-25

16. Each of the following materials is commonly used as sheet metal flashing for roof water-   16._____
    proofing EXCEPT

    A. lead   B. galvanized steel
    C. copper   D. zinc

17. The MOST commonly used type of metal lath for wall support is   17._____

    A. self-furring   B. flat rib
    C. flat diamond mesh   D. 3/8" rib

18. Approximately how long will it take to install a non-mortised lockset?   18._____

    A. 15 minutes   B. 30 minutes
    C. 1 hour   D. 2 hours

19. What is represented by the architectural symbol shown at   19._____
    the right?

    A. Cut stone   B. Concrete block
    C. Rubble stone   D. Brick

20. What type of nails are typically used for installing floor sheathing?   20._____

    A. 4d   B. 8d   C. 12d   D. 16d

21. Each of the following is considered *finish* electrical work EXCEPT

    A. outlet boxes
    B. light fixtures
    C. connection of fixtures to wiring
    D. switches

22. Which component of cost estimating typically presents the GREATEST difficulty?

    A. Materials
    B. Overhead
    C. Profit
    D. Labor

23. Approximately how many hours will it take to install and caulk a typical sliding shower door assembly?

    A. 2   B. 4   C. 6   D. 8

24. What is represented by the electrical symbol shown at the right?

    A. Single pole switch
    B. Lock or key switch
    C. Service weather head
    D. Main switch

25. Approximately how many exterior square feet can one painter cover, applying a primer coat and two coats of finish paint, in an average work day?

    A. 100   B. 250   C. 350   D. 500

KEY (CORRECT ANSWERS)

1.	D		11.	B
2.	B		12.	D
3.	C		13.	B
4.	B		14.	C
5.	B		15.	C
6.	C		16.	A
7.	A		17.	C
8.	B		18.	B
9.	B		19.	A
10.	B		20.	B

21. A
22. D
23. B
24. A
25. D

TEST 3

DIRECTIONS: Each question or incomplete statement is followed by several suggested answers or completions. Select the one that BEST answers the question or completes the statement. *PRINT THE LETTER OF THE CORRECT ANSWER IN THE SPACE AT THE RIGHT.*

1. Irregular shapes and narrow lites typically reduce the rate of glass installation by _____%.
   A. 10-20   B. 25-35   C. 30-50   D. 55-75

2. What is represented by the electrical symbol shown at the right?
   A. Exposed wiring   B. Fusible element
   C. Three-way switch   D. Circuit breaker

3. Approximately how many square feet of siding can be installed by a crew in a typical work day?
   A. 250   B. 500   C. 750   D. 1,000

4. What is the construction term for hinges used on doors?
   A. Gables   B. Butts   C. Hips   D. Plates

5. Floor joists are typically spaced about _____ apart.
   A. 16"   B. 2 feet   C. 3 feet   D. 4 feet

6. Which of the following paving materials is generally MOST expensive?
   A. Brick on sand bed   B. Random flagstone
   C. Asphalt   D. Concrete

7. Approximately how long should it take a 2-person crew to install floor joists for a 100 square-foot area of floor space?
   A. 30 minutes   B. 1 hour
   C. 3 hours   D. 1 work day

8. A _____ is represented by the mechanical symbol shown at the right.
   A. pressure-reducing valve B. motor-operated valve
   C. lock and shield valve   D. globe valve

9. On average, labor costs for a job will be about _____% of the total job cost.
   A. 15   B. 35   C. 55   D. 85

10. Most exterior paint averages a coverage of about _____ square feet per gallon.
    A. 100   B. 250   C. 400   D. 550

11. What type of window includes two sashes which slide vertically?

    A. Double-hung B. Screen
    C. Casement   D. Sliding

12. Approximately how many linear feet of drywall tape can be applied during an average work day?

    A. 250 B. 400 C. 750 D. 1,000

13. What is used to join lengths of copper pipe?

    A. Molten solder
    B. Threaded ends and sealer
    C. Nipples
    D. Lead-and-oakum seal

14. Typically, one gallon of prepared wallpaper paste will supply adhesive for _____ full rolls of wall covering.

    A. 8 B. 12 C. 24 D. 36

15. What is represented by the electrical symbol shown at the right?

    A. Range outlet
    B. Wall bracket light fixture
    C. Split-wired receptacle
    D. Special purpose outlet

16. What size is MOST wire used in residential work?

    A. 6 B. 8 C. 12 D. 16

17. Most fire codes require fire-resistant floor underneath fireplace units which extends to at least _____ inches beyond the unit.

    A. 6 B. 12 C. 18 D. 24

18. If a building is constructed without a basement, _____ are typically used as footings.

    A. joists   B. staked caissons
    C. grade beams   D. mud sills

19. What is the MOST commonly used size range for flashing and gutter sheet metal?

    A. 8-12 B. 14-18 C. 22-26 D. 24-30

20. Approximately how many square feet of interior wall space can one painter, using a brush, cover in an hour?

    A. 25-50 B. 100 C. 175-200 D. 250

21. Which of the following downspout materials would be MOST expensive?

    A. Copper   B. Aluminum
    C. Zinc   D. Stainless steel

22. What is represented by the mechanical symbol shown at the right? 22._____

    A. Expansion valve   B. Floor drain
    C. Shower   D. Scale trap

23. Approximately how much lead (pounds) is required per joint in one sewer line lead-and- oakum seal? 23._____

    A. 1/4   B. 1/2   C. 1 1/2   D. 3

24. Which of the following caulking materials is MOST expensive? 24._____

    A. Neoprene   B. Butyl
    C. Polyurethane   D. Latex

25. The assembly inside a tank toilet that controls the water supply is the 25._____

    A. P trap   B. bell-and-spigot
    C. gating   D. ball cock

KEY (CORRECT ANSWERS)

1.	C	11.	A
2.	B	12.	A
3.	A	13.	A
4.	B	14.	B
5.	A	15.	C
6.	D	16.	C
7.	C	17.	B
8.	D	18.	C
9.	A	19.	C
10.	C	20.	B

21. A
22. A
23. A
24. B
25. C

WORK SCHEDULING

EXAMINATION SECTION
TEST 1

DIRECTIONS: Each question or incomplete statement is followed by several suggested answers or completions. Select the one that BEST answers the question or completes the statement. *PRINT THE LETTER OF THE CORRECT ANSWER IN THE SPACE AT THE RIGHT.*

Questions 1-6.

DIRECTIONS: Questions 1 through 6 are to be answered SOLELY on the basis of the information given in the ELEVATOR OPERATORS' WORK SCHEDULE shown below.

\multicolumn{5}{c}{ELEVATOR OPERATORS' WORK SCHEDULE}
Operator	Hours of Work	A.M. Relief Period	Lunch Hour	P.M. Relief Period
Anderson	8:30-4:30	10:20-10:30	12:00-1:00	2:20-2:30
Carter	8:00-4:00	10:10-10:20	11:45-12:45	2:30-2:40
Daniels	9:00-5:00	10:20-10:30	12:30-1:30	3:15-3:25
Grand	9:30-5:30	11:30-11:40	1:00-2:00	4:05-4:15
Jones	7:45-3:45	9:45-9:55	11:30-12:30	2:05-2:15
Lewis	9:45-5:45	11:40-11:50	1:15-2:15	4:20-4:30
Nance	8:45-4:45	10:50-11:00	12:30-1:30	3:05-3:15
Perkins	8:00-4:00	10:00-10:10	12:00-1:00	2:40-2:50
Russo	7:45-3:45	9:30-9:40	11:30-12:30	2:10-2:20
Smith	9:45-5:45	11:45-11:55	1:15-2:15	4:05-4:15

1. The two operators who are on P.M. relief at the SAME time are

   A. Anderson and Daniels B. Carter and Perkins
   C. Jones and Russo D. Grand and Smith

   1.____

2. Of the following, the two operators who have the SAME lunch hour are

   A. Anderson and Perkins B. Daniels and Russo
   C. Grand and Smith D. Nance and Russo

   2.____

3. At 12:15, the number of operators on their lunch hour is

   A. 3 B. 4 C. 5 D. 6

   3.____

4. The operator who has an A.M. relief period right after Perkins and a P.M. relief period right before Perkins is

   A. Russo B. Nance C. Daniels D. Carter

   4.____

5. The number of operators who are scheduled to be working at 4:40 is

   A. 5 B. 6 C. 7 D. 8

   5.____

6. According to the schedule, it is MOST correct to say that

   A. no operator has a relief period during the time that another operator has a lunch hour
   B. each operator has to wait an identical amount of time between the end of lunch and the beginning of P.M. relief period
   C. no operator has a relief period before 9:45 or after 4:00
   D. each operator is allowed a total of 1 hour and 20 minutes for lunch hour and relief periods

KEY (CORRECT ANSWERS)

1. D
2. A
3. C
4. D
5. A
6. D

TEST 2

DIRECTIONS: Each question or incomplete statement is followed by several suggested answers or completions. Select the one that BEST answers the question or completes the statement. *PRINT THE LETTER OF THE CORRECT ANSWER IN THE SPACE AT THE RIGHT.*

Questions 1-7.

DIRECTIONS: Questions 1 through 7 are to be answered SOLELY on the basis of the time sheet and instructions given below.

The following time sheet indicates the times that seven laundry workers arrived and left each day for the week of August 23. The times they arrived for work are shown under the heading IN, and the times they left are shown under the heading OUT. The letter (P) indicates time which was used for personal business. Time used for this purpose is charged to annual leave. Lunch time is one-half hour from noon to 12:30 P.M. and is not accounted for on this time record.

The employees on this shift are scheduled to work from 8:00 A.M. to 4:00 P.M. Lateness is charged to annual leave. Reporting after 8:00 A.M. is considered late.

	MON.		TUES.		WED.		THURS.		FRI.	
	AM IN	PM OUT	AM IN	PM OUT	AM IN	PM OUT	AM IN	PM OUT	AM IN	PM OUT
Baxter	7:50	4:01	7:49	4:07	8:00	4:07	8:20	4:00	7:42	4:03
Gardner	8:02	4:00	8:20	4:00	8:05	3:30(P)	8:00	4:03	8:00	4:07
Clements	8:00	4:04	8:03	4:01	7:59	4:00	7:54	4:06	7:59	4:00
Tompkins	7:56	4:00	Annual leave		8:00	4:07	7:59	4:00	8:00	4:01
Wagner	8:04	4:03	7:40	4:00	7:53	4:04	8:00	4:09	7:53	4:00
Patterson	8:00	2:30(P)	8:15	4:04	Sick leave		7:45	4:00	7:59	4:04
Cunningham	7:43	4:02	7:50	4:00	7:59	4:02	8:00	4:10	8:00	4:00

1. Which one of the following laundry workers did NOT have any time charged to annual leave or sick leave during the week?

    A. Gardner   B. Clements   C. Tompkins   D. Cunningham

2. On which day did ALL the laundry workers arrive on time?

    A. Monday   B. Wednesday   C. Thursday   D. Friday

3. Which of the following laundry workers used time to take care of personal business?

    A. Baxter and Clements   B. Patterson and Cunningham
    C. Gardner and Patterson   D. Wagner and Tompkins

4. How many laundry workers were late on Monday?

    A. 1   B. 2   C. 3   D. 4

5. Which one of the following laundry workers arrived late on three of the five days?

    A. Baxter   B. Gardner   C. Wagner   D. Patterson

137

6. The percentage of laundry workers reporting to work late on Tuesday is MOST NEARLY 6._____

   A. 15% B. 25% C. 45% D. 50%

7. The percentage of laundry workers that were absent for an entire day during the week is MOST NEARLY 7._____

   A. 6% B. 9% C. 15% D. 30%

KEY (CORRECT ANSWERS)

1. D
2. D
3. C
4. B
5. B
6. C
7. D

TEST 3

Questions 1-9.

DIRECTIONS: Questions 1 through 9 are to be answered SOLELY on the basis of the following information and timesheet given below.

The following is a foreman's timesheet for his crew for one week. The hours worked each day or the reason the man was off on that day are shown on the sheet. *R* means rest day. *A* means annual leave. *S* means sick leave. Where a man worked only part of a day, both the number of hours worked and the number of hours taken off are entered. The reason for absence is entered in parentheses next to the number of hours taken off.

Name	Saturday	Sunday	Monday	Tuesday	Wednesday	Thursday	Friday
Smith	R	R	7	7	7	3 4(A)	7
Jones	R	7	7	7	7	7	R
Green	R	R	7	7	S	S	S
White	R	R	7	7	A	7	7
Doe	7	7	7	7	7	R	R
Brown	R	R	A	7	7	7	7
Black	R	R	S	7	7	7	7
Reed	R	R	7	7	7	7	S
Roe	R	R	A	7	7	7	7
Lane	7	R	R	7	7	A	S

1. The caretaker who worked EXACTLY 21 hours during the week is

    A. Lane B. Roe C. Smith D. White

2. The TOTAL number of hours worked by all caretakers during the week is

    A. 268 B. 276 C. 280 D. 288

3. The two days of the week on which MOST caretakers were off are

    A. Thursday and Friday B. Friday and Saturday
    C. Saturday and Sunday D. Sunday and Monday

4. The day on which three caretakers were off on sick leave is

    A. Monday B. Friday C. Saturday D. Sunday

5. The two workers who took LEAST time off during the week are

    A. Doe and Reed B. Jones and Doe
    C. Reed and Smith D. Smith and Jones

6. The caretaker who worked the LEAST number of hours during the week is

    A. Brown B. Green C. Lane D. Roe

7. The caretakers who did NOT work on Thursday are

    A. Doe, White, and Smith
    B. Green, Doe, and Lane
    C. Green, Doe, and Smith
    D. Green, Lane, and Smith

8. The day on which one caretaker worked ONLY 3 hours is 8._____
   A. Friday   B. Saturday   C. Thursday   D. Wednesday

9. The day on which ALL caretakers worked is 9._____
   A. Monday   B. Thursday   C. Tuesday   D. Wednesday

KEY (CORRECT ANSWERS)

1. A
2. B
3. C
4. B
5. B
6. B
7. B
8. C
9. C

TEST 4

Questions 1-6.

DIRECTIONS: Questions 1 through 6 are to be answered SOLELY on the basis of the table below which shows the initial requests made by staff for vacation. It is to be used with the RULES AND GUIDELINES to make the decisions and judgments called for in each of the questions.

VACATION REQUESTS FOR THE ONE YEAR PERIOD FROM MAY 1, YEAR X THROUGH APRIL 30, YEAR Y				
Name	Work Assignment	Date Appointed	Accumulated Annual Leave Days	Vacation Periods Requested
DeMarco	MVO	Mar. 2003	25	May 3-21; Oct. 25-Nov. 5
Moore	Dispatcher	Dec. 1997	32	May 24-June 4; July 12-16
Kingston	MVO	Apr. 2007	28	May 24-June 11; Feb. 7-25
Green	MVO	June 2006	26	June 7-18; Sept. 6-24
Robinson	MVO	July 2008	30	June 28-July 9; Nov. 15-26
Reilly	MVO	Oct. 2009	23	July 5-9; Jan. 31-Mar. 3
Stevens	MVO	Sept. 1996	31	July 5-23; Oct. 4-29
Costello	MVO	Sept. 1998	31	July 5-30; Oct. 4-22
Maloney	Dispatcher	Aug. 1992	35	July 5-Aug. 6; Nov. 1-5
Hughes	Director	Feb. 1990	38	July 26-Sept. 3
Lord	MVO	Jan. 2010	20	Aug. 9-27; Feb. 7-25
Diaz	MVO	Dec. 2009	28	Aug. 9-Sept. 10
Krimsky	MVO	May 2006	22	Oct. 18-22: Nov. 22-Dec. 10

RULES AND GUIDELINES

1. The two Dispatchers cannot be on vacation at the same time, nor can a Dispatcher be on vacation at the same time as the Director.

2. For the period June 1 through September 30, not more than three MVO's can be on vacation at the same time.

3. For the period October 1 through May 31, not more than two MVO's at a time can be on vacation.

4. In cases where the same vacation time is requested by too many employees for all of them to be given the time under the rules, the requests of those who have worked the longest will be granted.

5. No employee may take more leave days than the number of annual leave days accumulated and shown in the table.

6. All vacation periods shown in the table and described in the questions below begin on a Monday and end on a Friday.

7. Employees work a five-day week (Monday through Friday). They are off weekends and holidays with no charges to leave balances. When a holiday falls on a Saturday or Sunday, employees are given the following Monday off without charge to annual leave.

8. Holidays: May 31   October 25   January 1
              July 4   November 2   February 12
              September 6   November 25   February 21
              October 11   December 25   February 21

9. An employee shall be given any part of his initial requests that is permissible under the above rules and shall have first right to it despite any further adjustment of schedule.

---

1. Until adjustments in the vacation schedule can be made, the vacation dates that can be approved for Krimsky are

    A. Oct. 18-22; Nov. 22-Dec. 10
    B. Oct. 18-22; Nov. 29-Dec. 10
    C. Oct. 18-22 *only*
    D. Nov. 22-Dec. 10 *only*

2. Until adjustments in the vacation schedule can be made, the vacation dates that can be approved for Maloney are

    A. July 5-Aug. 6; Nov. 1-5
    B. July 5-23; Nov. 1-5
    C. July 5-9; Nov. 1-5
    D. Nov. 1-5 *only*

3. According to the table, Lord wants a vacation in August and another in February. Until adjustments in the vacation schedule can be made, he can be allowed to take _____ of the August vacation and _____ of the February vacation.

    A. all; none   B. all; almost half
    C. almost all; almost half   D. almost half; all

4. Costello cannot be given all the vacation he has requested because

    A. the MVO's who have more seniority than he has have requested time he wishes
    B. he does not have enough accumulated annual leave
    C. a dispatcher is applying for vacation at the same time as Costello
    D. there are five people who want vacation in July

5. According to the table, how many leave days will DeMarco be charged for his vacation from October 25 through November 5?

    A. 10   B. 9   C. 8   D. 7

6. How many leave days will Moore use if he uses the requested vacation allowable to him under the rules?

    A. 9   B. 10   C. 14   D. 15

KEY (CORRECT ANSWERS)

1. D
2. B
3. A
4. B
5. C
6. A

TEST 5

Questions 1-8.

DIRECTIONS: Questions 1 through 8 are to be answered SOLELY on the basis of Charts I, II, III, and IV. Assume that you are the supervisor of Operators R, S, T, U, V, W, and X, and it is your responsibility to schedule their lunch hours.

The charts each represent a possible scheduling of lunch hours during a lunch period from 11:30 - 2:00. An operator-hour is one hour of time spent by one operator. Each box on the chart represents one half-hour. The boxes marked L represent the time when each operator is scheduled to have her lunch hour. For example, in Chart I, next to Operator R, the boxes for 11:30 - 12:00 and 12:00 -12:30 are marked L. This means that Operator R is scheduled to have her lunch hour from 11:30 to 12:30.

I

	11:30-12:00	12:00-12:30	12:30-1:00	1:00-1:30	1:30-2:00
R	L	L			
S		L	L		
T		L	L		
U			L	L	
V			L	L	
W				L	L
X				L	L

II

	11:30-12:00	12:00-12:30	12:30-1:00	1:00-1:30	1:30-2:00
R				L	L
S		L	L		
T	L	L			
U		L	L		
V				L	L
W				L	L
X		L	L		

III

	11:30-12:00	12:00-12:30	12:30-1:00	1:00-1:30	1:30-2:00
R	L	L			
S				L	L
T	L	L			
U			L	L	
V	L	L			
W				L	L
X				L	L

IV

	11:30-12:00	12:00-12:30	12:30-1:00	1:00-1:30	1:30-2:00
R	L	L			
S	L	L			
T		L	L		
U			L	L	
V				L	L
W				L	L
X			L	L	

1. If, under the schedule represented in Chart II, Operator R has her lunch hour changed to 12:30-1:30, that leaves how many operator-hours of phone coverage from 1:00-2:00?

   A. 2   B. 2 1/2   C. 3   D. 4 1/2

2. If Operator S asks you whether she and Operator T may have the same lunch hour, you could accommodate her by using the schedule in Chart

   A. I   B. II   C. III   D. IV

3. From past experience you know that the part of the lunch period when the phones are busiest is from 12:30-1:30. Which chart shows the BEST phone coverage from 12:30 to 1:30?

   A. I   B. II   C. III   D. IV

4. At least three operators have the same lunch hour according to Chart(s)

   A. II and III   B. II and IV
   C. III only   D. IV only

144

5. Which chart would provide the POOREST phone coverage during the period 12:00-1:30, based on total number of operator-hours from 12:00 to 1:30?

    A. I   B. II   C. III   D. IV

6. Which chart would make it possible for U, W, and X to have the same lunch hour?

    A. I   B. II   C. III   D. IV

7. The portion of the lunch period during which the telephones are least busy is 11:30-12:30.
   Which chart is MOST likely to have been designed with that fact in mind?

    A. I   B. II   C. III   D. IV

8. Assume that you have decided to use Chart IV to schedule your operators' lunch hours on a specific day. Operator T asks you if she can have her lunch hour changed to 1:00-2:00.
   If you grant her request, how many operators will be working during the period 12:00 to 12:30?

    A. 1   B. 2   C. 4   D. 5

KEY (CORRECT ANSWERS)

1. D
2. A
3. B
4. A
5. A

6. C
7. C
8. D

TEST 6

Questions 1-13.

DIRECTIONS: Questions 1 through 13 consist of a statement. You are to indicate whether the statement is TRUE (T) or FALSE (F). *PRINT THE LETTER OF THE CORRECT ANSWER IN THE SPACE AT THE RIGHT.* Questions 1 through 13 are to be answered SOLELY on the basis of the information given in the table below.

\multicolumn{6}{c}{DEPARTMENT OF FERRIES}

Name	Year Employed	Ferry Assigned	Hours of Work	Lunch Period	Days Off
Adams	1999	Hudson	7 AM - 3 PM	11-12	Fri. and Sat.
Baker	1992	Monroe	7 AM - 3 PM	11-12	Sun. and Mon.
Gunn	1995	Troy	8 AM - 4 PM	12-1	Fri. and Sat.
Hahn	1989	Erie	9 AM - 5 PM	1-2	Sat. and Sun.
King	1998	Albany	7 AM - 3 PM	11-12	Sun. and Mon.
Nash	1993	Hudson	11 AM - 7 PM	3-4	Sun. and Mon.
Olive	2003	Fulton	10 AM - 6 PM	2-3	Sat. and Sun.
Queen	2002	Albany	11 AM - 7 PM	3-4	Fri. and Sat.
Rose	1990	Troy	11 AM - 7 PM	3-4	Sun. and Mon.
Smith	1991	Monroe	10 AM - 6 PM	2-3	Fri. and Sat.

1. The chart shows that there are only five (5) ferries being used.   1.____

2. The attendant who has been working the LONGEST time is Rose.   2.____

3. The Troy has one more attendant assigned to it than the Erie.   3.____

4. Two (2) attendants are assigned to work from 10 P.M. to 6 A.M.   4.____

5. According to the chart, no more than one attendant was hired in any year.   5.____

6. The NEWEST employee is Olive.   6.____

7. There are as many attendants on the 7 to 3 shift as on the 11 to 7 shift.   7.____

8. MOST of the attendants have their lunch either between 12 and 1 or 2 and 3.   8.____

9. All the employees work four (4) hours before they go to lunch.   9.____

10. On the Hudson, Adams goes to lunch when Nash reports to work.   10.____

11. All the attendants who work on the 7 to 3 shift are off on Saturday and Sunday.   11.____

12. All the attendants have either a Saturday or Sunday as one of their days off.   12.____

13. At least two (2) attendants are assigned to each ferry.   13.____

2 (#6)

KEY (CORRECT ANSWERS)

1. F   6. T   11. F
2. F   7. T   12. T
3. T   8. F   13. F
4. F   9. T
5. T   10. T

REPORT WRITING

EXAMINATION SECTION

TEST 1

DIRECTIONS: Each question or incomplete statement is followed by several suggested answers or completions. Select the one that BEST answers the question or completes the statement. *PRINT THE LETTER OF THE CORRECT ANSWER IN THE SPACE AT THE RIGHT.*

1. Following are six steps that should be taken in the course of report preparation:
   I. Outlining the material for presentation in the report
   II. Analyzing and interpreting the facts
   III. Analyzing the problem
   IV. Reaching conclusions
   V. Writing, revising, and rewriting the final copy
   VI. Collecting data

   According to the principles of good report writing, the CORRECT order in which these steps should be taken is:
   A. VI, III, II, I, IV, V
   B. III, VI, II, IV, I, V
   C. III, VI, II, I, IV, V
   D. VI, II, III, IV, I, V

   1.____

2. Following are three statements concerning written reports:
   I. Clarity is generally more essential in oral reports than in written reports.
   II. Short sentences composed of simple words are generally preferred to complex sentences and difficult words.
   III. Abbreviations may be used whenever they are customary and will not distract the attention of the reader.

   Which of the following choices correctly classifies the above statements in to those which are valid and those which are not valid?
   A. I and II are valid, but III is not valid
   B. I is valid, but II and III are not valid.
   C. II and III are valid, but I is not valid.
   D. III is valid, but I and II are not valid.

   2.____

3. In order to produce a report written in a style that is both understandable and effective, an investigator should apply the principles of unit, coherence, and emphasis.
   The one of the following which is the BEST example of the principle of coherence is
   A. interlinking sentences so that thoughts flow smoothly
   B. having each sentence express a single idea to facilitate comprehension
   C. arranging important points in prominent positions so they are not overlooked
   D. developing the main idea fully to insure complete consideration

   3.____

4. Assume that a supervisor is preparing a report recommending that a standard work procedure be changed.
Of the following, the MOST important information that he should include in this report is
   A. a complete description of the present procedure
   B. the details and advantages of the recommended procedure
   C. the type and amount of retraining needed
   D. the percentage of men who favor the change

5. When you include in your report on an inspection some information which you have obtained from other individuals, it is MOST important that
   A. this information have no bearing on the work these other people are performing
   B. you do not report as fact the opinions of other individuals
   C. you keep the source of the information confidential
   D. you do not tell the other individuals that their statements will be included in your report

6. Before turning in a report of an investigator of an accident, you discover some additional information you did not know about when you wrote the report.
Whether or not you re-write your report to include this additional information should depend MAINLY on the
   A. source of this additional information
   B. established policy covering the subject matter of the report
   C. length of the report and the time it would take you to re-write it
   D. bearing this additional information will have on the conclusions in the report

7. The MOST desirable *first* step in the planning of a written report is to
   A. ascertain what necessary information is readily available in the files
   B. outline the methods you will employ to get the necessary information
   C. determine the objectives and uses of the report
   D. estimate the time and cost required to complete the report

8. In writing a report, the practice of taking up the least important points and the most important points last is a
   A. *good* technique since the final points made in a report will make the greatest impression on the reader
   B. *good* technique since the material is presented in a more logical manner and will lead directly to the conclusions
   C. *poor* technique since the reader's time is wasted by having to review irrelevant information before finishing the report
   D. *poor* technique since it may cause the reader to lose interest in the report and arrive at incorrect conclusions about the report

9. Which one of the following serves as the BEST guideline for you to follow for effective written reports?
   Keep sentences
   A. short and limit sentences to one thought
   B. short and use as many thoughts as possible
   C. long and limit sentences to one thought
   D. long and use as many thoughts as possible

9.____

10. One method by which a supervisor might prepare written reports to management is to begin with the conclusions, results, or summary, and to follow this with the supporting data.
    The BEST reason why management may *prefer* this form of report is that
    A. management lacks the specific training to understand the data
    B. the data completely supports the conclusions
    C. time is saved by getting to the conclusions of the report first
    D. the data contains all the information that is required for making the conclusions

10.____

11. When making written reports, it is MOST important that they be
    A. well-worded
    B. accurate as to the facts
    C. brief
    D. submitted immediately

11.____

12. Of the following, the MOST important reason for a supervisor to prepare good written reports is that
    A. a supervisor is rated on the quality of his reports
    B. decisions are often made on the basis of the reports
    C. such reports take less time for superiors to review
    D. such reports demonstrate efficiency of department operations

12.____

13. Of the following, the BEST test of a good report is whether it
    A. provides the information needed
    B. shows the good sense of the writer
    C. is prepared according to a proper format
    D. is grammatical and neat

13.____

14. When a supervisor writes a report, he can BEST show that he has a understanding of the subject of the report by
    A. including necessary facts and omitting nonessential details
    B. using statistical data
    C. giving his conclusions but not the data on which they are based
    D. using a technical vocabulary

14.____

15. Suppose you and another supervisor on the same level are assigned to work together on a report. You disagree strongly with one of the recommendations the other supervisor wants to include in the report but you cannot change his views.

15.____

Of the following, it would be BEST that
- A. you refuse to accept responsibility for the report
- B. you ask that someone else be assigned to this project to replace you
- C. each of you state his own ideas about this recommendation in the report
- D. you give in to the other supervisor's opinion for the sake of harmony

16. Standardized forms are often provided for submitting reports. 16.____
Of the following, the MOST important advantage of using standardized forms for reports is that
- A. they take less time to prepare than individually written reports
- B. the person making the report can omit information he considers unimportant
- C. the responsibility for preparing these reports can be turned over to subordinates
- D. necessary information is less likely to be omitted

17. A report which may BEST be classed as a *periodic* report is one which 17.____
- A. requires the same type of information at regular intervals
- B. contains detailed information which is to be retained in permanent records
- C. is prepared whenever a special situation occurs
- D. lists information in graphic form

18. In the writing of reports or letters, the ideas presented in a paragraph are usually 18.____
of unequal importance and require varying degrees of emphasis.
All of the following are methods of placing extra stress on an idea EXCEPT
- A. repeating it in a number of forms
- B. placing it in the middle of the paragraph
- C. placing it either at the beginning or at the end of a paragraph
- D. underlining it

Questions 19-25.

DIRECTIONS: Questions 19 through 25 concern the subject of report writing and are based on the information and incidents described in the following paragraph. (In answering these questions, assume that the facts and incidents in the paragraph are true.)

On December 15, at 8 A.M., seven Laborers reported to Foreman Joseph Meehan in the Greenbranch Yard in Queens. Meehan instructed the men to load some 50-pound boxes of books on a truck for delivery to an agency building in Brooklyn. Meehan told the men that, because the boxes were rather heavy, two men should work together, helping each other lift and load each box. Since Michael Harper, one of the Laborers, was without a partner, Meehan helped him with the boxes for a while. When Meehan was called to the telephone in a nearby building, however, Harper decided to lift a box himself. He appeared able to lift the box, but, as he got the box halfway up, he cried out that he had a sharp pain in his back. Another Laborer, Jorge Ortiz, who was passing by, ran over to help Harper put the box down. Harper suddenly dropped the box, which fell on Ortiz' right foot. By this time, Meehan had come out of the building. He immediately helped get the box off Ortiz' foot and had both men lie down. Meehan covered the men with blankets and called an ambulance, which arrived a half hour later. At the hospital, the doctor said that the X-ray results showed that Ortiz' right foot was broken in three places.

19. What would be the BEST term to use in a report describing the injury of Jorge Ortiz?
    A. Strain   B. Fracture   C. Hernia   D. Hemorrhage

19.____

20. Which of the following would be the MOST accurate summary for the Foreman to put in his report of the incident?
    A. Ortiz attempted to help Harper carry a box which was too heavy for one person, but Harper dropped it before Ortiz got there.
    B. Ortiz tried to help Harper carry a box but Harper got a pain in his back and accidentally dropped the box on Ortiz' foot.
    C. Harper refused to follow Meehan's orders and lifted a box too heavy for him; he deliberately dropped it when Ortiz tried to help him carry it.
    D. Harper lifted a box and felt a pain in his back; Ortiz tried to help Harper put the box down but Harper accidentally dropped it on Ortiz' foot.

20.____

21. One of the Laborers at the scene of the accident was asked his version of the incident.
Which information obtained from this witness would be LEAST important for including in the accident report?
    A. His opinion as to the cause of the accident
    B. How much of the accident he saw
    C. His personal opinion of the victims
    D. His name and address

21.____

22. What should be the MAIN objective of writing a report about the incident described in the above paragraph? To
    A. describe the important elements in the accident situation
    B. recommend that such Laborers as Ortiz be advised not to interfere in another's work unless given specific instructions
    C. analyze the problems occurring when there are not enough workers to perform a certain task
    D. illustrate the hazards involved in performing routine everyday tasks

22.____

23. Which of the following is information *missing* from the above passage but which *should* be included in a report of the incident? The
    A. name of the Laborer's immediate supervisor
    B. contents of the boxes
    C. time at which the accident occurred
    D. object or action that caused the injury to Ortiz' foot

23.____

24. According to the description of the incident, the accident occurred because
    A. Ortiz attempted to help Harper who resisted his help
    B. Harper failed to follow instructions given him by Meehan
    C. Meehan was not supervising his men as closely as he should have
    D. Harper was not strong enough to carry the box once he lifted it

24.____

25. Which of the following is MOST important for a foreman to avoid when writing up an official accident report?
    A. Using technical language to describe equipment involved in the accident
    B. Putting in details which might later be judged unnecessary
    C. Giving an opinion as to conditions that contributed to the accident
    D. Recommending discipline for employees who, in his opinion, caused the accident

---

KEY (CORRECT ANSWERS)

1.	B		11.	B
2.	C		12.	B
3.	A		13.	A
4.	B		14.	A
5.	B		15.	C
6.	D		16.	D
7.	C		17.	A
8.	D		18.	B
9.	A		19.	B
10.	C		20.	D

21.	C
22.	A
23.	C
24.	B
25.	D

TEST 2

DIRECTIONS: Each question or incomplete statement is followed by several suggested answers or completions. Select the one that BEST answers the question or completes the statement. *PRINT THE LETTER OF THE CORRECT ANSWER IN THE SPACE AT THE RIGHT.*

1. Lieutenant X is preparing a report to submit to his commanding officer in order to get approval of a plan of operation he has developed.
   The report starts off with the statement of the problem and continues with the details of the problem. It contains factual information gathered with the help of field and operational personnel. It contains a final conclusion and recommendation for action. The recommendation is supplemented by comments from other precinct staff members on how the recommendations will affect their areas of responsibility. The report also includes directives and general orders ready for the commanding officer's signature. In addition, it has two statements of objections presented by two precinct staff members.
   Which one of the following, if any, is either an item that Lieutenant X should have included in his report and which is not mentioned above, or is an item which Lieutenant X improperly did include in his report?
    A. Considerations of alternative courses of action and their consequences should have been covered in the report.
    B. The additions containing undocumented objections to the recommended course of action should not have been included as part of the report.
    C. A statement on the qualifications of Lieutenant X, which would support his expertness in the field under consideration, should have been included in the report.
    D. The directives and general orders should not have been prepared and included in the report until the commanding officer had approved the recommendations.
    E. None of the above, since Lieutenant X's report was both proper and complete.

1.____

2. During a visit to a section, the district supervisor criticizes the method being used by the assistant foreman to prepare a certain report and orders him to modify the method. This change ordered by the district supervisor is in direct conflict with the specific orders of the foreman.
   In this situation, it would be BEST for the assistant foreman to
    A. change the method and tell the foreman about the change at the first opportunity
    B. change the method and rely on the district supervisor to notify the foreman
    C. report the matter to the foreman and delay the preparation of the report
    D. ask the district supervisor to discuss the matter with the foreman but use the old method for the time being

2.____

3. A department officer should realize that the MOST usual reason for writing a report is to
   A. give orders and follow up their execution
   B. establish a permanent record
   C. raise questions
   D. supply information

4. A very important report which is being prepared by a department officer will soon be due on the desk of the district supervisor. No typing help is available at this time for the officer.
   For the officer to write out this report in longhand in such a situation would be
   A. *bad*; such a report would not make the impression a typed report would
   B. *good*; it is important to get the report in on time
   C. *bad*; the district supervisor should not be required to read longhand reports
   D. *good*; it would call attention to the difficult conditions under which this section must work

5. In a well-written report, the length of each paragraph in the report should be
   A. varied according to the content
   B. not over 300 words
   C. pretty nearly the same
   D. gradually longer as the report is developed and written

6. A clerk in the headquarters office complains to you about the way in which you are filing out a certain report.
   It would be BEST for you to
   A. tell the clerk that you are following official procedures in filling out the report
   B. ask to be referred to the clerk's superior
   C. ask the clerk exactly what is wrong with the way in which you are filling out the report
   D. tell the clerk that you are following the directions of the district supervisor

7. The use of an outline to help in writing a report is
   A. *desirable*, in order to insure good organization and coverage
   B. *necessary*, so it can be used as an introduction to the report itself
   C. *undesirable*, since it acts as a straightjacket and may result in an unbalanced report
   D. *desirable*, if you know your immediate supervisor reads reports with extreme care and attention

8. It is advisable that a department officer do his paper work and report writing as soon as he has completed an inspection MAINLY because
   A. there are usually deadlines to be met
   B. it insures a steady work-flow
   C. he may not have time for this later
   D. the facts are then freshest in his mind

9. Before you turn in a report you have written of an investigation that you have made, you discover some additional information you didn't know about before. Whether or not you re-write the report to include this additional information should depend MAINLY on the
    A. amount of time remaining before the report is due
    B. established policy of the department covering the subject matter of the report
    C. bearing this information will have on the conclusions of the report
    D. number of people who will eventually review the report

9._____

10. When a supervisory officer submits a periodic report to the district supervisor, he should realize that the CHIEF importance of such a report is that it
    A. is the principal method of checking on the efficiency of the supervisor and his subordinates
    B. is something to which frequent reference will be made
    C. eliminates the need for any personal follow-up or inspection by higher echelons
    D. permits the district supervisor to exercise his functions of direction, supervision, and control better

10._____

11. Conclusions and recommendations are usually placed at the end rather than at the beginning of a report because
    A. the person preparing the report may decide to change some of the conclusions and recommendations before he reaches the end of the report
    B. they are the most important part of the report
    C. they can be judged better by the person to whom the report is sent after he reads the facts and investigators which come earlier in the report
    D. they can be referred to quickly when needed without reading the rest of the report

11._____

12. The use of the same method of record-keeping and reporting by all agency sections is
    A. *desirable*, MAINLY because it saves time in section operations
    B. *undesirable*, MAINLY because it kills the initiative of the individual section foreman
    C. *desirable*, MAINLY because it will be easier for the administrator to evaluate and compare section operations
    D. *undesirable*, MAINLY because operations vary from section to section and uniform record-keeping and reporting is not appropriate

12._____

13. The GREATEST benefit the section officer will have from keeping complete and accurate records and reports of section operations is that
    A. he will find it easier to run his section efficiently
    B. he will need less equipment
    C. he will need less manpower
    D. the section will run smoothly when he is out

13._____

14. You have prepared a report to your superior and are ready to send it forward. 14.____
But on re-reading it, you think some parts are not clearly expressed and your
superior ay have difficulty getting your point.
Of the following, it would be BEST for you to
    A. give the report to one of your men to read, and if he has no trouble
       understanding it send it through
    B. forward the report and call your superior the next day to ask whether it
       was all right
    C. forward the report as is; higher echelons should be able to understand
       any report prepared by a section officer
    D. do the report over, re-writing the sections you are in doubt about

15. The BEST of the following statements concerning reports is that 15.____
    A. a carelessly written report may give the reader an impression of
       inaccuracy
    B. correct grammar and English are unimportant if the main facts are given
    C. every man should be required to submit a daily work report
    D. the longer and more wordy a report is, the better it will read

16. In writing a report, the question of whether or not to include certain material 16.____
could be determined BEST by considering the
    A. amount of space the material will occupy in the report
    B. amount of time to be spent in gathering the material
    C. date of the material
    D. value of the material to the superior who will read the report

17. Suppose you are submitting a fairly long report to your superior. 17.____
The one of the following sections that should come FIRST in this report is a
    A. description of how you gathered material
    B. discussion of possible objections to your recommendations
    C. plan of how your recommendations can be put into practice
    D. statement of the problem dealt with

Questions 18-20.

DIRECTIONS: A foreman is asked to write a report on the incident described in the following
             passage. Answer Questions 18 through 20 based on the following information.

On March 10, Henry Moore, a laborer, was in the process of transferring some equipment from the machine shop to the third floor. He was using a dolly to perform this task and, as he was wheeling the material through the machine shop, laborer Bob Greene called to him. As Henry turned to respond to Bob, he jammed the dolly into Larry Mantell's leg, knocking Larry down in the process and causing the heavy drill that Larry was holding to fall on Larry's foot. Larry started rubbing his foot and then, infuriated, jumped up and punched Henry in the jaw. The force of the blow drove Henry's head back against the wall. Henry did not fight back; he appeared to be dazed. An ambulance was called to take Henry to the hospital, and the ambulance attendant told the foreman that it appeared likely that Henry had suffered a concussion. Larry's injuries consisted of some bruises, but he refused medical attention.

18. An adequate report of the above incident should give as minimum information the names of the persons involved, the names of the witnesses, the date and the time that each event took place, and the
    A. names of the ambulance attendants
    B. names of all the employees working in the machine shop
    C. location where the accident occurred
    D. nature of the previous safety training each employee had been given

18.____

19. The only one of the following which is NOT a fact is
    A. Bob called to Henry
    B. Larry suffered a concussion
    C. Larry rubbed his foot
    D. the incident took place in the machine shop

19.____

20. Which of the following would be the MOST accurate summary of the incident for the foreman to put in his report of the accident?
    A. Larry Mantell punched Henry Moore because a drill fell on his foot and he was angry. Then Henry fell and suffered a concussion.
    B. Henry Moore accidentally jammed a dolly into Larry Mantell's foot, knocking Larry down. Larry punched Henry, pushing him into the wall and causing him to bang his head against the wall.
    C. Bob Greene called Henry Moore. A dolly than jammed into Larry Mantell and knocked him down. Larry punched Henry who tripped and suffered some bruises. An ambulance was called.
    D. A drill fell on Larry Mantell's foot. Larry jumped up suddenly and punched Henry Moore and pushed him into the wall. Henry may have suffered a concussion as a result of falling.

20.____

Questions 21-25.

DIRECTIONS: Questions 21 through 25 are to be answered ONLY on the basis of the information provided in the following passage.

A written report is a communication of information from one person to another. It is an account of some matter especially investigated, however routine that matter may be. The ultimate basis of any good written report is facts, which become known through observation and verification. Good written reports may seem to be no more than general ideas and opinions. However, in such cases, the facts leading to these opinions were gathered, verified, and reported earlier, and the opinions are dependent upon these facts. Good style, proper form, and emphasis cannot make a good written report out of unreliable information and bad judgment; but, on the other hand, solid investigation and brilliant thinking are not likely to become very useful until they are effectively communicated to others. If a person's work calls for written reports, then his work is often no better than his written reports.

6 (#2)

21. Based on the information in the above passage, it can be concluded that opinions expressed in a report should be
    A. based on facts which are gathered and reported
    B. emphasized repeatedly when they result from a special investigation
    C. kept to a minimum
    D. separated from the body of the report

    21.____

22. In the above passage, the one of the following which is mentioned as a way of establishing facts is
    A. authority
    B. communication
    C. reporting
    D. verification

    22.____

23. According to the above passage, the characteristic shared by ALL written reports is that they are
    A. accounts of routine matters
    B. transmissions of information
    C. reliable and logical
    D. written in proper form

    23.____

24. Which of the following conclusions can logically be drawn from the information given in the above passage?
    A. Brilliant thinking can make up for unreliable information in a report.
    B. One method of judging an individual's work is the quality of the written reports he is required to submit.
    C. Proper form and emphasis can make a good report out of unreliable information.
    D. Good written reports that seem to be no more than general ideas should be rewritten.

    24.____

25. Which of the following suggested titles would be MOST appropriate for this passage?
    A. Gathering and Organizing Facts
    B. Techniques of Observation
    C. Nature and Purpose of Reports
    D. Reports and Opinions: Differences and Similarities

    25.____

KEY (CORRECT ANSWERS)

1. A
2. A
3. D
4. B
5. A

6. C
7. A
8. D
9. C
10. D

11. C
12. C
13. A
14. D
15. A

16. D
17. D
18. C
19. B
20. B

21. A
22. D
23. B
24. B
25. C

TEST 3

DIRECTIONS: Each question or incomplete statement is followed by several suggested answers or completions. Select the one that BEST answers the question or completes the statement. *PRINT THE LETTER OF THE CORRECT ANSWER IN THE SPACE AT THE RIGHT.*

Questions 1-5.

DIRECTIONS: The following is an accident report similar to those used in departments for reporting accidents. Questions 1 through 5 are be answered using ONLY the information given in this report.

ACCIDENT REPORT

FROM: John Doe	DATE OF REPORT: June 23
TITLE: Sanitation Worker	
DATE OF ACCIDENT: June 22 time 3 AM PM	CITY: Metropolitan
PLACE: 1489 Third Avenue	
VEHICLE NO. 1	**VEHICLE NO. 2**
OPERATOR: John Doe, Sanitation Worker Title	OPERATOR: Richard Roe
VEHICLE CODE NO: 14-238	ADDRESS: 498 High Street
LICENSE NO.: 0123456	OWNER: Henry Roe ADDRESS: 786 E.83 St. LIC. NO.: 5N1492
DESCRIPTION OF ACCIDENT: Light green Chevrolet sedan while trying to pass drove in to rear side of sanitation truck which had stopped to collect garbage. No one was injured but there was property damage.	
NATURE OF DAMAGE TO PRIVATE VEHICLE: Right front fender crushed, bumper bent	
DAMAGE TO CITY VEHICLE: Front of left rear fender pushed in. Paint scraped.	
NAME OF WITNESS: Frank Brown	ADDRESS: 48 Kingsway
SIGNATURE OF PERSON MAKING THIS REPORT *John Doe*	BADGE NO.: 428

1. Of the following, the one which has been omitted from this accident report is the
    A. location of the accident
    B. drivers of the vehicles involved
    C. traffic situation at the time of the accident
    D. owners of the vehicles involved

1._____

2. The address of the driver of Vehicle No. 1 is not required because he
    A. is employed by the department
    B. is not the owner of the vehicle
    C. reported the accident
    D. was injured in the accident

2._____

3. The report indicates that the driver of Vehicle No. 2 was PROBABLY
    A. passing on the wrong side of the truck
    B. not wearing his glasses
    C. not injured in the accident
    D driving while intoxicated

3._____

4. The number of people *specifically* referred to in this report is 4._____
   A. 3   B. 4   C. 5   D. 6

5. The license number of Vehicle No. 1 is 5._____
   A. 428   B. 5N1492   C. 14-238   D. 0123456

6. In a report of unlawful entry into department premises, it is LEAST important to include the 6._____
   A. estimated value of the property missing
   B. general description of the premises
   C. means used to get into the premises
   D. time and date of entry

7. In a report of an accident, it is LEAST important to include the 7._____
   A. name of the insurance company of the person injured in the accident
   B. probable cause of the accident
   C. time and place of the accident
   D. names and addresses of all witnesses of the accident

8. Of the following, the one which is NOT required in the preparation of a weekly functional expense report is the 8._____
   A. hourly distribution of the time by proper heading in accordance with the actual work performed
   B. signatures of officers not involved in the preparation of the report
   C. time records of the men who appear on the payroll of the respective locations
   D. time records of men working in other districts assigned to this location

KEY (CORRECT ANSWERS)

1. C   5. D
2. A   6. B
3. C   7. A
4. B   8. B

GLOSSARY OF PROJECT MANAGEMENT

A

Agile software development is a set of fundamental principles about how software should be developed based on an agile way of working in contrast to previous heavy-handed software development methodologies.

Aggregate planning is an operational activity which does an aggregate plan for the production process, in advance of 2 to 18 months, to give an idea to management as to what quantity of materials and other resources are to be procured and when, so that the total cost of operations of the organization is kept to the minimum over that period.

Allocation is the assignment of available resources in an economic way.

B

Budget generally refers to a list of all planned expenses and revenues.

Budgeted cost of work performed (BCWP) measures the budgeted cost of work that has actually been performed, rather than the cost of work scheduled.

Budgeted cost of work scheduled (BCWS) the approved budget that has been allocated to complete a scheduled task (or Work Breakdown Structure (WBS) component) during a specific time period.

Business model is a profit-producing system that has an important degree of independence from the other systems within an enterprise.

Business analysis is the set of tasks, knowledge, and techniques required to identify business needs and determine solutions to business problems. Solutions often include a systems development component, but may also consist of process improvement or organizational change.

Business operations are those ongoing recurring activities involved in the running of a business for the purpose of producing value for the stakeholders. They are contrasted with project management, and consist of business processes.

Business process is a collection of related, structured activities or tasks that produce a specific service or product (serve a particular goal) for a particular customer or customers. There are three types of business processes: Management processes, Operational processes, and Supporting processes.

Business Process Modeling (BPM) is the activity of representing processes of an enterprise, so that the current ("as is") process may be analyzed and improved in future ("to be").

C

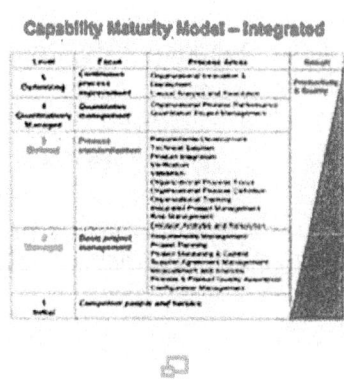

Capability Maturity Model.

Capability Maturity Model (CMM) in software engineering is a model of the maturity of the capability of certain business processes. A maturity model can be described as a structured collection of elements that describe certain aspects of maturity in an organization, and aids in the definition and understanding of an organization's processes.

Change control is the procedures used to ensure that changes (normally, but not necessarily, to IT systems) are introduced in a controlled and coordinated manner. Change control is a major aspect of the broader discipline of change management.

Change management is a field of management focused on organizational changes. It aims to ensure that methods and procedures are used for efficient and prompt handling of all changes to controlled IT infrastructure, in order to minimize the number and impact of any related incidents upon service.

Case study is a research method which involves an in-depth, longitudinal examination of a single instance or event: a case. They provide a systematic way of looking at events, collecting data, analyzing information, and reporting the results.

Certified Associate in Project Management is an entry-level certification for project practitioners offered by Project Management Institute.

Communications Log is an on-going documentation of communication events between any identified project stakeholders, managed and collected by the project manager that describes: the sender and receiver of the communication event; where, when and for how long the communication event elapsed; in what form the communication event took place; a summary of what information was communicated; what actions/outcomes should be taken as a result of the communication event; and to what level of priority should the actions/outcomes of the communication event be graded

Constructability is a project management technique to review the construction processes from start to finish during pre-construction phrase. It will identify obstacles before a project is actually built to reduce or prevent error, delays, and cost overrun.

Costs in economics, business, and accounting are the value of money that has been used up to produce something, and hence is not available for use anymore. In business, the cost may be one of acquisition, in which case the amount of money expended to acquire it is counted as cost.

Cost engineering is the area of engineering practice where engineering judgment and experience are used in the application of scientific principles and techniques to problems of cost estimating, cost control, business planning and management science, profitability analysis, project management, and planning and scheduling."[

Construction, in the fields of architecture and civil engineering, is a process that consists of the building or assembling of infrastructure. Far from being a single activity, large scale construction is a feat of multitasking. Normally the job is managed by the project manager and supervised by the construction manager, design engineer, construction engineer or project architect.

Cost overrun is defined as excess of actual cost over budget.

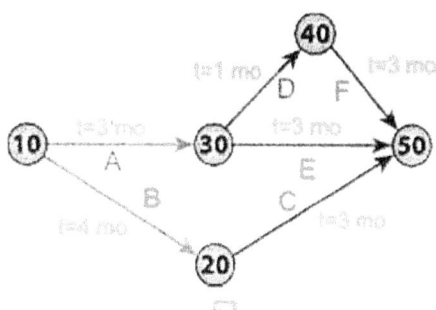

PERT chart with two critical paths.

Critical path method (CPM) is a mathematically based modeling technique for scheduling a set of project activities, used in project management.

Critical chain project management (CCPM) is a method of planning and managing projects that puts more emphasis on the resources required to execute project tasks.

D

Dependency in a project network is a link amongst a project's terminal elements.

Dynamic Systems Development Method (DSDM) is a software development methodology originally based upon the Rapid Application Development methodology. DSDM is an iterative and incremental approach that emphasizes continuous user involvement.

Duration of a project's terminal element is the number of calendar periods it takes from the time the execution of element starts to the moment it is completed.

Deliverable A contractually required work product, produced and delivered to a required state. A deliverable may be a document, hardware, software or other tangible product.

E

Earned schedule (ES) is an extension to earned value management (EVM), which renames two traditional measures, to indicate clearly they are in units of currency or quantity, not time.

Earned value management (EVM) is a project management technique for measuring project progress in an objective manner, with a combination of measuring scope, schedule, and cost in a single integrated system.

Effort management is a project management subdiscipline for effective and efficient use of time and resources to perform activities regarding quantity, quality and direction.

Enterprise modeling is the process of understanding an enterprise business and improving its performance through creation of enterprise models. This includes the modelling of the relevant business domain (usually relatively stable), business processes (usually more volatile), and Information technology

Estimation in project management is the processes of making accurate estimates using the appropriate techniques.

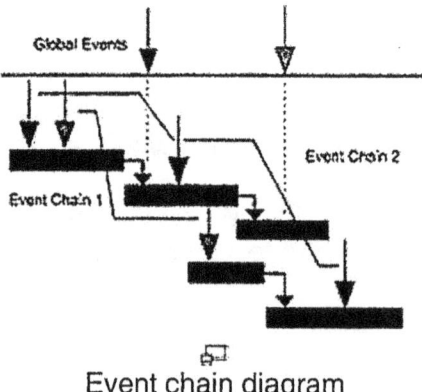
Event chain diagram

Event chain diagram : diagram that show the relationships between events and tasks and how the events affect each other.

Event chain methodology is an uncertainty modeling and schedule network analysis technique that is focused on identifying and managing events and event chains that affect project schedules.

Extreme project management (XPM) refers to a method of managing very complex and very uncertain projects.

F

Float in a project network is the amount of time that a task in a project network can be delayed without causing a delay to subsequent tasks and or the project completion date.

Focused Improvement in Theory of Constraints is the ensemble of activities aimed at elevating the performance of any system, especially a business system, with respect to its goal by eliminating its constraints one by one and by not working on non-constraints.

Fordism, named after Henry Ford, refers to various social theories. It has varying but related meanings in different fields, and for Marxist and non-Marxist scholars.

G

Henry Gantt was an American mechanical engineer and management consultant, who developed the Gantt chart in the 1910s.

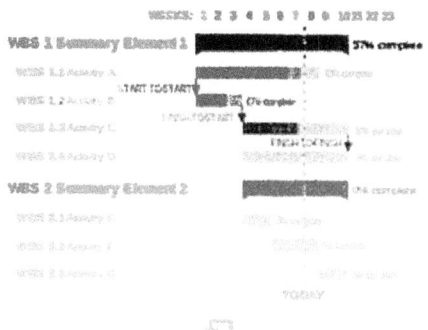

A Gantt chart.

Gantt chart is a type of bar chart that illustrates a project schedule. It illustrate the start and finish dates of the terminal elements and summary elements of a project. Terminal elements and summary elements comprise the work breakdown structure of the project.

Goal or objective consists of a projected state of affairs which a person or a system plans or intends to achieve or bring about — a personal or organizational desired end-point in some sort of assumed development. Many people endeavor to reach goals within a finite time by setting deadlines

Goal setting involves establishing specific, measurable and time targeted objectives

Graphical Evaluation and Review Technique (GERT) is a network analysis technique that allows probabilistic treatment of both network logic and activity duration estimated.

H

Hammock activity is a grouping of subtasks that "hangs" between two end dates it is tied to (or the two end-events it is fixed to).

HERMES is a Project Management Method developed by the Swiss Government, based on the German V-Modell. The first domain of application was software projects.

I

Integrated Master Plan (IMP) is an event-based, top level plan, consisting of a hierarchy of Program Events.

ISO 10006 is a guidelines for quality management in projects, is an international standard developed by the International Organization for Standardization.

Iterative and Incremental development is a cyclic software development process developed in response to the weaknesses of the waterfall model. It starts with an initial planning and ends with deployment with the cyclic interaction in between

K

Kickoff meeting is the first meeting with the project team and the client of the project.

L

Level of Effort (LOE) is qualified as a support type activity which doesn't lend itself to measurement of a discrete accomplishment. Examples of such an activity may be project budget accounting, customer liaison, etc.

Linear scheduling method (LSM) is a graphical scheduling method focusing on continuous resource utilization in repetitive activities. It is believed that it originally adopted the idea of Line-Of-Balance method.

Lean manufacturing or lean production, which is often known simply as "Lean", is the practice of a theory of production that considers the expenditure of resources for any means other than the creation of value for the presumed customer to be wasteful, and thus a target for elimination.

M

Management in business and human organization activity is simply the act of getting people together to accomplish desired goals. Management comprises planning, organizing, staffing, leading or directing, and controlling an organization (a group of one or more people or entities) or effort for the purpose of accomplishing a goal.

Management process is a process of planning and controlling the performance or execution of any type of activity.

Management science (MS), is the discipline of using mathematical modeling and other analytical methods, to help make better business management decisions.

Megaproject is an extremely large-scale investment project.

Motivation is the set of reasons that prompts one to engage in a particular behavior.

N

Nonlinear Management (NLM) is a superset of management techniques and strategies that allows order to emerge by giving organizations the space to self-organize, evolve and adapt, encompassing Agile, Evolutionary and Lean approaches, as well as many others.

O

Operations management is an area of business that is concerned with the production of good quality goods and services, and involves the responsibility of ensuring that business operations are efficient and effective. It is the management of resources, the distribution of goods and services to customers, and the analysis of queue systems.

Operations, see **Business operations**

Operations Research (OR) is an interdisciplinary branch of applied mathematics and formal science that uses methods such as mathematical modeling, statistics, and algorithms to arrive at optimal or near optimal solutions to complex problems.

Organization is a social arrangement which pursues collective goals, which controls its own performance, and which has a boundary separating it from its environment.

Organization development (OD) is a planned, structured, organization-wide effort to increase the organization's effectiveness and health.

P

Planning in organizations and public policy is both the organizational process of creating and maintaining a plan; and the psychological process of thinking about the activities required to create a desired goal on some scale.

Portfolio in finance is an appropriate mix of or collection of investments held by an institution or a private individual.

PRINCE2 : PRINCE2 is a project management methodology. The planning, monitoring and control of all aspects of the project and the motivation of all those involved in it to achieve the project objectives on time and to the specified cost, quality and performance.

Process is an ongoing collection of activities, with an inputs, outputs and the energy required to transform inputs to outputs.

Process architecture is the structural design of general process systems and applies to fields such as computers (software, hardware, networks, etc.), business processes (enterprise architecture, policy and procedures, logistics, project management, etc.), and any other process system of varying degrees of complexity.

Process management is the ensemble of activities of planning and monitoring the performance of a process, especially in the sense of business process, often confused with reengineering.

Product breakdown structure (PBS) in project management is an exhaustive, hierarchical tree structure of components that make up an item, arranged in whole-part relationship.

Product description in project management is a structured format of presenting information about a project product

Program Evaluation and Review Technique (PERT) is a statistical tool, used in project management, designed to analyze and represent the tasks involved in completing a given project.

Program Management is the process of managing multiple ongoing inter-dependent projects. An example would be that of designing, manufacturing and providing support infrastructure for an automobile manufacturer.

Project : A temporary endeavor undertaken to create a unique product, service, or result.

Project accounting Is the practice of creating financial reports specifically designed to track the financial progress of projects, which can then be used by managers to aid project management.

Project Cost Management A method of managing a project in real-time from the estimating stage to project control; through the use of technology cost, schedule and productivity is monitored.

Project management : The complete set of tasks, techniques, tools applied during project execution'.

Project Management Body of Knowledge (PMBOK) : The sum of knowledge within the profession of project management that is standardized by ISO.

Project management office: The Project management office in a business or professional enterprise is the department or group that defines and maintains the standards of process, generally related to project management, within the organization. The PMO strives to standardize and introduce economies of repetition in the execution of projects. The PMO is the source of documentation, guidance and metrics on the practice of project management and execution.

Project management process is the management process of planning and controlling the performance or execution of a project.

Project Management Professional is a certificated professional in project management.

Project Management Simulators are computer-based tools used in project management training programs. Usually, project management simulation is a group exercise. The computer-based simulation is an interactive learning activity.

Project management software is a type of software, including scheduling, cost control and budget management, resource allocation, collaboration software, communication, quality management and documentation or administration systems, which are used to deal with the complexity of large projects.

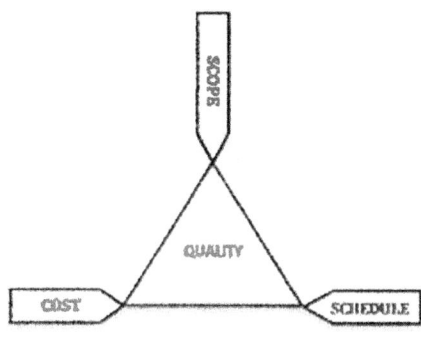

Project Management Triangle

Project Management Triangle is a model of the constraints of project management.

Project manager : professional in the field of project management. Project managers can have the responsibility of the planning, execution, and closing of any project, typically relating to construction industry, architecture, computer networking, telecommunications or software development.

Project network is a graph (flow chart) depicting the sequence in which a project's terminal elements are to be completed by showing terminal elements and their dependencies.

Project plan is a formal, approved document used to guide both *project execution* and *project control*. The primary uses of the project plan are to document planning assumptions and decisions, facilitate communication among *stakeholders*, and document approved scope, cost, and schedule *baselines*. A project plan may be summary or detailed.

Project planning is part of project management, which relates to the use of schedules such as Gantt charts to plan and subsequently report progress within the project environment.

Project stakeholders are those entities within or without an organization which sponsor a project or, have an interest or a gain upon a successful completion of a project.

Project team is the management team leading the project, and provide services to the project. Projects often bring together a variety number of problems. Stakeholders have important issues with others.

Proport refers to the combination of the unique skills of an organisation's members for collective advantage.

Q

Quality can mean a high degree of excellence ("a quality product"), a degree of excellence or the lack of it ("work of average quality"), or a property of something ("the addictive quality of alcohol").[1] Distinct from the vernacular, the subject of this article is the business interpretation of quality.

Quality, Cost, Delivery(QCD) as used in lean manufacturing measures a businesses activity and develops Key performance indicators. QCD analysis often forms a part of continuous improvement programs

R

Reengineering is radical redesign of an organization's processes, especially its business processes. Rather than organizing a firm into functional specialties (like production, accounting, marketing, etc.) and considering the tasks that each function performs; complete processes from materials acquisition, to production, to marketing and distribution should be considered. The firm should be re-engineered into a series of processes.

Resources are what is required to carry out a project's tasks. They can be people, equipment, facilities, funding, or anything else capable of definition (usually other than labour) required for the completion of a project activity.

Risk is the precise probability of specific eventualities.

Risk management is a management specialism aiming to reduce different risks related to a preselected domain to the level accepted by society. It may refer to numerous types of threats caused by environment, technology, humans, organizations and politics.

Risk register is a tool commonly used in project planning and organizational risk assessments.

S

Schedules in project management consists of a list of a project's terminal elements with intended start and finish dates.

Scientific management is a theory of management that analyzes and synthesizes workflow processes, improving labor productivity.

Scope of a project in project management is the sum total of all of its products and their requirements or features.

Scope creep refers to uncontrolled changes in a project's scope. This phenomenon can occur when the scope of a project is not properly defined, documented, or controlled. It is generally considered a negative occurrence that is to be avoided.

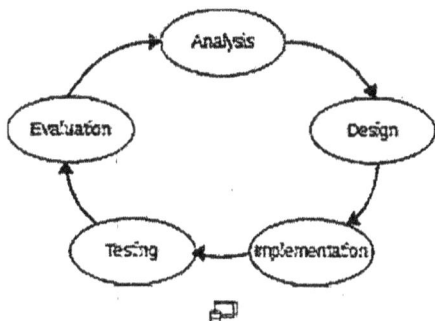

The systems development life cycle.

Scrum is an iterative incremental process of software development commonly used with agile software development. Despite the fact that "Scrum" is not an acronym, some companies implementing the process have been known to adhere to an all capital letter expression of the word, i.e. SCRUM.

Six Sigma is a business management strategy, originally developed by Motorola, that today enjoys widespread application in many sectors of industry.

Software engineering is the application of a systematic, disciplined, quantifiable approach to the development, operation, and maintenance of software.[1]

Systems Development Life Cycle (SDLC) is any logical process used by a systems analyst to develop an information system, including requirements, validation, training, and user ownership. An SDLC should result in a high quality system that meets or exceeds customer expectations, within time and cost estimates, works effectively and efficiently in the current and planned Information Technology infrastructure, and is cheap to maintain and cost-effective to enhance.

Systems engineering is an interdisciplinary field of engineering that focuses on how complex engineering projects should be designed and managed.

T

Task is part of a set of actions which accomplish a job, problem or assignment.

Tasks in project management are activity that needs to be accomplished within a defined period of time.

Task analysis is the analysis or a breakdown of exactly how a task is accomplished, such as what sub-tasks are required

Timeline is a graphical representation of a chronological sequence of events, also referred to as a chronology. It can also mean a schedule of activities, such as a timetable.

U

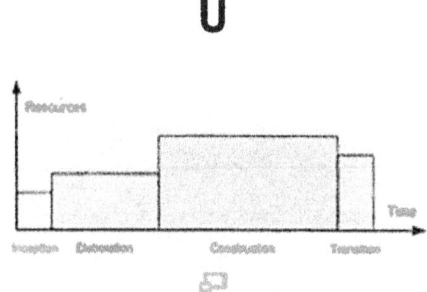

The Unified Process.

Unified Process: The Unified process is a popular iterative and incremental software development process framework. The best-known and extensively documented refinement of the Unified Process is the Rational Unified Process (RUP).

V

Value engineering (VE) is a systematic method to improve the "value" of goods and services by using an examination of function. Value, as defined, is the ratio of function to cost. Value can therefore be increased by either improving the function or reducing the cost. It is a primary tenet of value engineering that basic functions be preserved and not be reduced as a consequence of pursuing value improvements.

Vertical slice is a type of milestone, benchmark, or deadline, with emphasis on demonstrating progress across all components of a project.

Virtual Design and Construction (VDC) is the use of integrated multi-disciplinary performance models of design-construction projects, including the Product (i.e., facilities), Work Processes and Organization of the design - construction - operation team in order to support explicit and public business objectives.

W

Wideband Delphi is a consensus-based estimation technique for estimating effort.

Work in project management is the amount of effort applied to produce a deliverable or to accomplish a task (a terminal element).

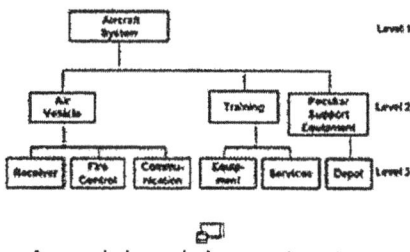
A work breakdown structure.

Work Breakdown Structure (WBS) is a tool that defines a project and groups the project's discrete work elements in a way that helps organize and define the total work scope of the project. A Work breakdown structure element may be a product, data, a service, or any combination. WBS also provides the necessary framework for detailed cost estimating and control along with providing guidance for schedule development and control.

Work package is a subset of a project that can be assigned to a specific party for execution. Because of the similarity, work packages are often misidentified as projects.

Workstream is a set of associated activities, focused around a particular scope that follow a path from initiation to completion.